Craft-a-Doodle Deux

Craft-a-Doodle Deux

73 Exercises for Creative Drawing

JENNY DOH

LARK
New York

LARK
New York

An Imprint of Sterling Publishing
1166 Avenue of the Americas
New York, NY 10036

ISBN 978-1-4547-0931-2

Distributed in Canada by Sterling Publishing
c/o Canadian Manda Group, 664 Annette Street
Toronto, Ontario, Canada M6S 2C8
Distributed in the United Kingdom by GMC Distribution Services
Castle Place, 166 High Street, Lewes, East Sussex, England BN7 1XU
Distributed in Australia by Capricorn Link (Australia) Pty. Ltd.
P.O. Box 704, Windsor, NSW 2756, Australia

For information about custom editions, special sales, and premium and corporate purchases,
please contact Sterling Special Sales at 800-805-5489 or specialsales@sterlingpublishing.com.

Manufactured in China

2 4 6 8 10 9 7 5 3 1

larkcrafts.com

CONTENTS

INTRODUCTION
by Jenny Doh

The thing I love most about doodling is that it is accessible to anyone. I also love that it's an activity that can be done practically anywhere … in the studio, in the car, in a restaurant, and my favorite … while on the phone.

Any pen or pencil will work, and paper of any sort will work: fancy watercolor paper, everyday copy paper, students' lined paper, junk mail, napkins, paint chip samples, envelopes, and on and on.

Of course there are ways to doodle that involve greater preparation, like the beautiful doodles that Julia Grimm teaches (page 44) by first drying flowers and then using the dried elements to make very unique doodles.

Everyday objects can also inspire remarkable doodles … like the ones that Javier Pérez Estrella shares (page 70). Whether it's a cookie or a coin or a piece of fruit, he shows us how to doodle unexpected and enchanting scenes with just a simple few lines of the pen.

In this book, *Craft-A-Doodle Deux*, 17 wonderful artists convene to offer more than 70 prompts and lessons that are sure to get your creative juices flowing! The contributing artists are **Jan Avellana**, **Jennifer Betlazar**, **Danita**, **David Danell**, **Theo Ellsworth**, **Monika Forsberg**, **Kate Gabrielle**, **Pam Garrison**, **Julia Grimm**, **Stephenie Purl Hamen**, **Lindsay Mason**, **Jennifer Mercede**, **Jen Osborn**, **Dino Perez**, **Javier Pérez Estrella**, **Heidi Vandal**, and yours truly.

This book is a sequel to the popular *Craft-A-Doodle*. It is exciting to continue providing projects that have been meticulously curated in order to inspire you on your very own doodling journey.

How to Use This Book

The beauty of doodling is that you don't need any time, money, or preparation to make it happen—it's one of the few art forms that requires next to no forethought! Of course you can doodle with loads of preparation, gather extensive materials of your choice, and spend hours on any given doodling project. But doodling is so refreshing because you don't *have* to do those things.

This book is filled with short prompts and exercises as well as lengthier, slightly more complex projects. There's no need to follow a certain order as you work through the book. When you have a free moment, pick an exercise at random and have fun with it!

For most of the projects in this book, you will only need paper of your choice and a writing utensil of your choice. Most of the artists suggest a slightly heavier weight paper and a pen to ensure that your work is more permanent, but whatever you have on hand and prefer will be great! For some of the slightly more involved projects, artists suggest using materials such as fine-point colored markers, permanent markers, and gel pens to add color. And some of the artists in this book even involve everyday items, such as paperclips or dried flowers, in their projects.

Regardless of the simplicity or complexity of the project, each exercise will include a mention or list of the materials the artist used. Feel free to use your own materials instead, or take inspiration from some of the materials they used to expand your artistic material collection.

Dig in to this book filled with creative and clever ideas for doodling, and let your imagination take the lead.

ARTSY Envelopes

DOODLE PROMPT: Turn mail into happy mail
with just a black marker!

what you'll need

- Plain white envelopes
- Black fine-point marker

instructions

1 On the front of an envelope, roughly in the middle, draw a large rounded box with a fine-point black marker. Write "To:" in the upper left-hand corner of the box.

2 Draw another rounded box in the upper left-hand corner of the envelope, and write "From:" in the corner of that box. Ⓐ

3 Working in sections, doodle your way across the rest of the envelope. Draw wavy and straight lines, stars, diamonds, teardrops, polka dots, and whatever else you like. Ⓑ

4 Turn the envelope over, lift up the flap, and doodle funky flowers on the portion of the inner envelope that you can see when it's opened. Ⓒ

tip

A variation of this idea would be to doodle on only part of the envelope. For instance, doodle only around the "To" and "From" boxes, or just along the bottom or back of the envelope.

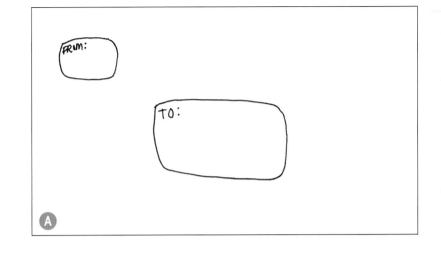

Ⓐ

Ⓑ

Ⓒ

Playing with PETALS

DOODLE PROMPT: Draw the garden of your dreams in this exercise. Make flower petals of all sizes with polka dots, stars, and diamonds!

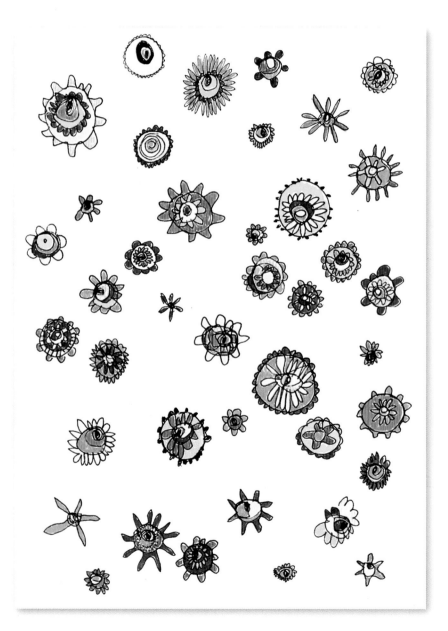

try it

On white paper, draw a small circle for the center of a flower with a black fine-point marker. Doodle rows of petals surrounding the circle, even multiple rows if you'd like! This is no time to worry about realism. Instead, push yourself to use dots, stars, and scallops as petals. Think thick, thin, fast, slow, wide, long, and push yourself outside of the usual flower box.

Fill an entire page with flowers and petals of all shapes and sizes. Let the ink dry, and then add color using gel pens in assorted colors.

NO-LIFT Doodling

DOODLE PROMPT: Here's your chance to freehand draw without thinking or planning anything beforehand. It's a great way to loosen up your hand and your creative juices. And there's only one rule—no lifting up your pen until you are finished!

try it

Press a black pen onto a piece of white paper, and start making lines and curves without picking up your pen. Don't try to make a certain shape, and instead let your hand go wherever it wants. Only pick up the pen when you've covered as much space as you'd like. If you're really feeling brave, try this exercise with your eyes closed!

Jennifer Mercede

BOLDLY PATTERNED
Butterflies

DOODLE PROMPT: Butterfly wings are what doodlers' dreams are made of—a blank canvas with the potential to be unique and beautiful.

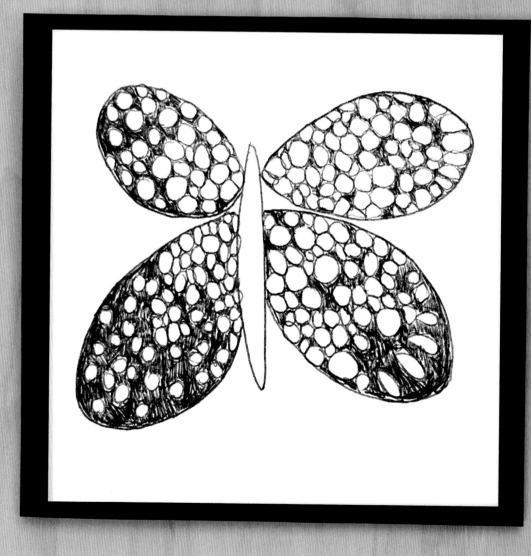

what you'll need

- Plain white paper
- Black fine-point marker

instructions

1 On white paper, use a black fine-point marker to draw the body of a butterfly with a thin, long, irregular oval. Ⓐ

2 Doodle the outline of butterfly wings by drawing four teardrop shapes stemming out from the body. Ⓑ

3 Doodle details within the constraints of the wings. You can pick one pattern such as polka dots for the entire butterfly (Ⓒ), or you can have several rows or sections of different doodles, such as stripes, scallops, petals, or dots. Ⓓ

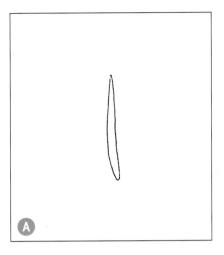

Ⓐ Ⓑ

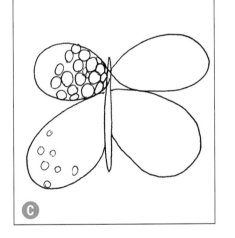

Ⓒ

tip

Try doodling different shapes for the butterfly wings. Perhaps the bottom two wings are really large compared to the top two, or perhaps the wings are shaped more like scallops or hearts.

Ⓓ

13

MR. FOX

DOODLE PROMPT: Follow these steps to doodle a friendly, colorful fox.

what you'll need

- Watercolor paper
- Black fine-point pigment liner
- Orange watercolor pencil
- Watercolor brush
- Small jar of water
- Black cardstock
- Adhesive
- Blank card

instructions

1 On watercolor paper, draw the basic outline of a fox with a black fine-point pigment liner. Ⓐ

2 Draw a zigzag line for the end of the tail and a partial oval for the chest patch. Ⓑ

3 Draw a partial triangle for the arm, and then doodle facial details, including dots for a nose and eyes and little triangles for inner ears. Ⓒ

4 Add glasses, accessories, flowers, hearts, and whatever details you'd like. Ⓓ

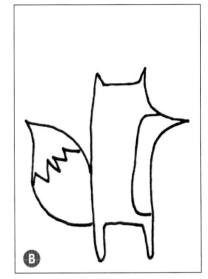

5 Let the ink dry, and then use an orange watercolor pencil to add color to the fox. Trim the doodled fox, and mount it onto a piece of black cardstock and trim. Attach the cardstock to the front of a blank card.

6 Use a watercolor brush and water to create gradients and spread the orange color. **E**

tip

After adding all the details with the liner, let the ink dry completely before adding the watercolors. This will keep the doodled lines sharp and clear.

Signature Doodle BUNNY

DOODLE PROMPT: I created this bunny as my signature doodle character. Since the shape is fairly basic, I like to customize each bunny using different outfits, accessories, and colors that represent my current mood or situation.

try it

Use a black gel pen to draw a circle for the head of the bunny and two oval shapes for the ears. Draw an oval body that is thinner but almost as tall as the head. Draw two small oval shapes for the legs, and then draw the arms close to where the head and body meet. Draw the inner ears and chest patch just inside the outer ovals. For the face, add two small circles for the eyes and a small X for the nose. Use a colored marker to add color to the inner ears and chest patch, and then personalize the bunny with accessories, such as glasses, bows, and jewelry. If you'd like, draw items such as a boat or a swim float to show an activity.

Family of DOLLS

DOODLE PROMPT: Matryoshka dolls, or nesting dolls as they're often called, date back to the 1800s in Russia, where woodworkers would craft them out of wood and intricately paint them. Doodling these dolls is a great way to play with patterns in a defined area.

what you'll need

- Plain white paper
- Black permanent marker
- Pink gel pen

instructions

1 On plain white paper, use a black permanent marker to draw a circle for the head and an oval for the body, keeping the body about 1.5 times the size of the head.

2 Draw a smaller circle inside the head for the face and two partial circles for the outline of the shawl. Ⓐ

3 Draw parted hair to shape the face. Add two small leaf shapes for the knot of the shawl, and draw a large U shape below it for the apron. Ⓑ

4 Draw the eyes and nose, and then use a pink gel pen to draw the rosy cheeks. Ⓒ

5 Doodle flowers, leaves, and polka dots to fill in the different areas of the body. Ⓓ (previous page) and Ⓔ

6 Make the patterns pop by filling in selected areas with a black permanent marker. Ⓕ

7 Draw a series of smaller and smaller dolls for a complete set of nesting dolls. Ⓖ

tip

- This is a fun exercise for kids on a rainy afternoon. Have kids doodle their own set of nesting dolls and then cut them out to play with.
- A full set of nesting dolls provides a perfect opportunity to have fun with color combinations. Add color to the face, the pattern shapes, or the areas behind the patterns.

Under the SEA

DOODLE PROMPT: Create a foundational character with just a few simple shapes and lines, and then personalize each mermaid with various patterns and outfits. Even the slightest difference will give each mermaid her own personality!

try it

Use a black fine-point marker to draw a circle for the mermaid's head, a curved shape for the body, and two irregular ovals for the tail. Draw arms, parted hair, and a crown. Decorate the tail and body with various patterns, such as petal shapes, or wavy or zigzag lines. Draw a bikini top, eyes, a nose, and a mouth, and add color to the cheeks using a pink gel pen.

FUNNY Faces

DOODLE PROMPT: Draw four unique faces by starting with the noses and working out from there. This slightly different approach to doodling a face is sure to fuel your creative juices.

what you'll need

- Plain white paper
- Black fine-point marker

instructions

1 On a piece of white paper, doodle a column of four distinct noses with a black fine-point marker.

2 Build onto the faces by doodling four distinct mouths and sets of eyes to go with each nose. Ⓐ

3 Draw a head shape around each set of facial features, and then add ears and hair if desired. Ⓑ

4 Doodle additional facial details, such as a mustache, wrinkles, or tears. Ⓒ

tip

Trace any shape or image with ease, and then let your creativity loose when you doodle within the shape. This approach provides a lot of freedom because it takes away the pressure of getting a main shape or character just right.

City of DOODLES

DOODLE PROMPT: A simple doodle becomes complex and interesting with just the right amount of repetition and layering.

try it

Using a black fine-point marker on white paper, doodle a dimensional building by drawing a rhombus for the roof and two vertical rectangular shapes for the front and side of the building. Draw tiny squares for the windows. Draw this same shape repeatedly, layering each new shape over an old one. Vary the buildings slightly by making some wider and some taller.

One-LINERS

DOODLE PROMPT: In this exercise, approach a group of everyday objects from two different doodling angles.

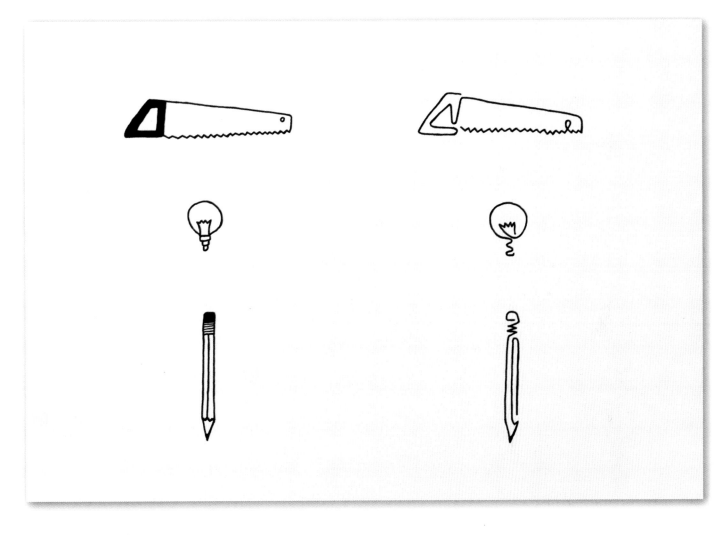

try it

On white paper, doodle a handsaw, a light bulb, and a pencil with a black fine-point marker, starting with the basic outlines and adding details and shaded areas to finish. Then draw the same objects again, but without lifting the pen off the paper so the doodle is one continuous line.

David Danell

EVERYDAY Doodles

DOODLE PROMPT: Doodling objects can seem intimidating, but when you approach it in three simple steps it's much more doable.

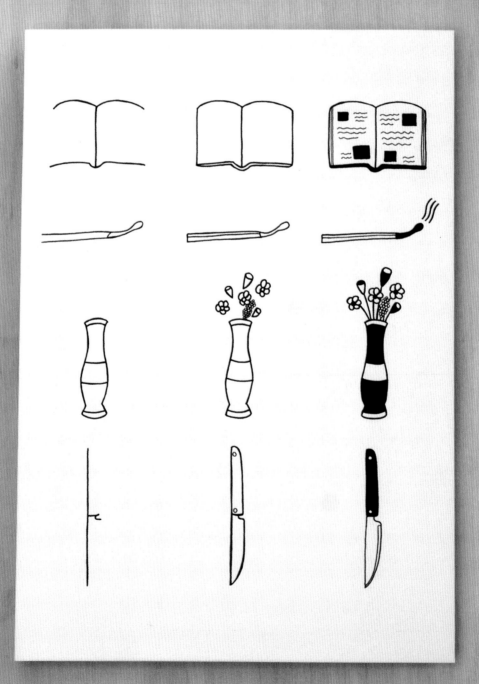

what you'll need

- Plain white paper
- Black fine-point marker

instructions

1 With a black fine-point marker on a white piece of paper, draw the bare outline of a book, a match, a vase, and a knife. Ⓐ

2 Finish each outline by making it a complete shape and adding the essential pieces, such as the pages of the book and the handle of the knife. Ⓑ

3 Add the details on each item, such as the flowers in the vase, the words and images on the book pages, and the smoke coming off the match. Ⓒ

tip

Drawing various objects around your house is great doodling practice. It not only gives you a chance to practice drawing, but it also allows you to find your own style of doodling.

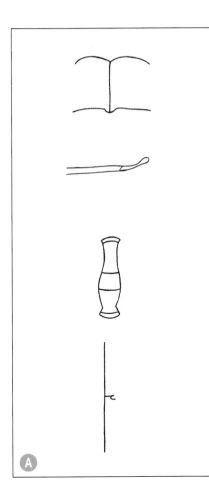

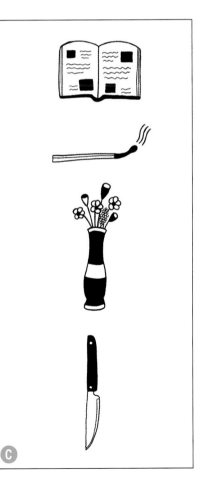

SINGLE-LINE Figures

DOODLE PROMPT: This fun exercise is good practice for letting loose and getting creative with what you have. I started by doodling a single line with lots of curls, loops, and direction changes, without trying to plan it out beforehand.

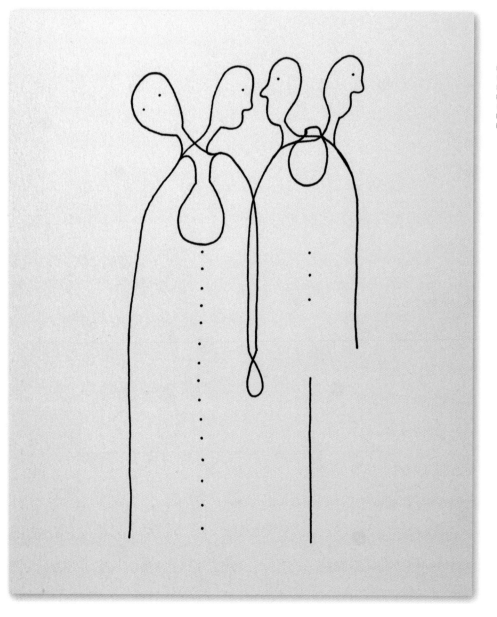

try it

Draw a single line with a black fine-point marker on a piece of white paper. You can doodle your own creative shape, or try this four-figured group, with a general focus on making two overlapping, tall rounded shapes. Add irregular necks and heads, dots for eyes, and lines made up of dots.

VISIONARY Flowers

DOODLE PROMPT: These big-eyed flowers feature doodled symbols that are meaningful to me—plus they're fun and pretty to boot!

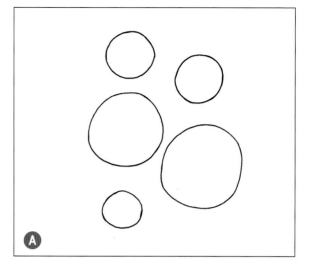

A

what you'll need

- Plain white paper
- Black fine-point marker
- Permanent markers in assorted colors

instructions

1 On a piece of white paper, use a black fine-point marker to draw five different-sized circles close to each other. **Ⓐ**

2 Around each circle, doodle petals of various styles and shapes. **Ⓑ**

3 Draw an eye in the middle of each circle. Within each pupil, draw a symbol that represents something important to you, such as a flower, a heart, a peace symbol, or a star.

4 Doodle eyelashes around each eye, made up of loops, diamonds, stars, or scallops.

5 Doodle around the inner edge of each circle with scallops, flowers, curlicues, and loops. **Ⓒ**

6 Add color and pattern to the petals with permanent markers.

B

tip

Try using a white gel pen to add contrast on some of the petals.

C

Doodles of a FEATHER

DOODLE PROMPT: In this exercise, learn to doodle wispy feathers with eye-catching designs.

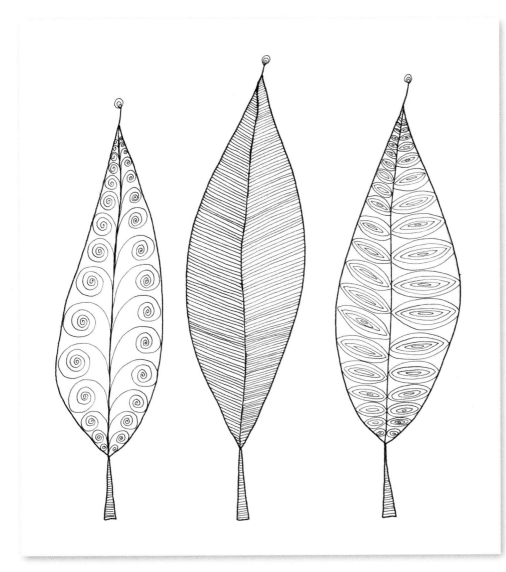

try it

On white paper, doodle three feather outlines with a black fine-point marker. Draw a line down the middle of each feather. Embellish each feather with different details such as curlicues, thin straight lines, or concentric ovals. Doodle thin horizontal lines within each stem, and draw a tiny curlicue at the top of each feather.

Jennifer Betlazar

FLOWER CAMEO Garland

DOODLE PROMPT: This happy garland is home to my three favorite fairy muses.

what you'll need

- Plain white paper
- Fine-point black marker
- Permanent markers in assorted colors

instructions

1 On white paper, draw three different-sized circles with a black fine-point marker. Doodle a loopy border at the top of the piece of paper. **Ⓐ**

2 Doodle petal shapes around each circle, varying the type and size of the petals for each one. Doodle loopy vines that connect the scalloped top border to each circle. **Ⓑ**

3 Draw a fairy character in each circle, starting with a circle for the head, two parallel lines for the neck, and a fun and fresh hairstyle for each one. **Ⓒ**

4 Doodle facial features on each creature.

5 Doodle embellished petals on the vines.

6 Add splashes of color with markers.

tips

- Try using different shapes to frame each one of the girls. You could turn the circles into sunshine shapes with triangles instead of petals, or you could start with a different shape altogether, such as a triangle or a wonky rectangle.
- Maybe your own personal muse is a different subject altogether. Consider drawing cute foxes, bears, or butterflies instead of fairy girls.

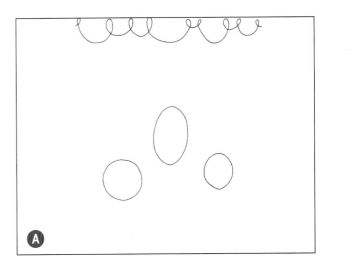

Ⓐ

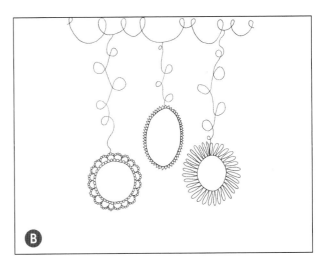

Ⓑ

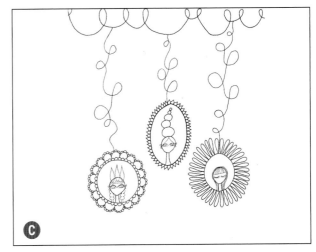

Ⓒ

Jennifer Betlazar

HEALING Hand

DOODLE PROMPT: This doodle starts with tracing your own hand, and ends with drawing symbols that are significant to you.

what you'll need

- Plain white paper
- Black fine-point marker

instructions

1 On a white piece of paper, trace the outline of your hand with a black fine-point marker. **Ⓐ**

2 Doodle a flower at the end of each fingertip **Ⓑ**, and then add an eye with a flower pupil at each first knuckle and a multi-layered diamond at each second knuckle. **Ⓒ**

3 Draw a large eye in the center of the palm, complete with loopy eyelashes. **Ⓓ**

4 Doodle flowers over the rest of the palm, and add a scalloped line to separate the palm from the fingers.

tip

The symbols on this hand are important and meaningful to me, so feel free to include symbols that are meaningful to you instead!

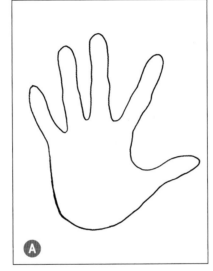

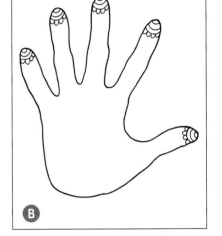

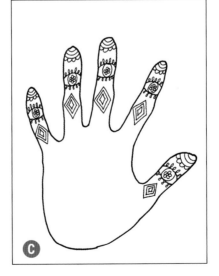

Jennifer Betlazar

A Home for FAIRIES

DOODLE PROMPT: This colorful home is the perfect abode for fairies, muses, or imaginary friends.

what you'll need

- Plain white paper
- Black fine-point marker
- Permanent markers in assorted colors

instructions

1 On plain white paper, use a black fine-point marker to draw three tall buildings with decorative tops right next to each other. Ⓐ

2 Doodle windows of various shapes and sizes on each building. Ⓑ

3 Draw the heads of fairies or imaginary friends in each window. Begin each character with a circle for the head, a long neck, big eyes, and a creative hairstyle. Ⓒ

4 Doodle embellishments for each building, such as thick stripes, polka dots, stars, or loopy lines.

5 Color in the fairies and the buildings with permanent markers.

tip

For a nice final touch, add a favorite quote or phrase down the side of one or more of the buildings.

PUZZLED Duck

DOODLE PROMPT: In this exercise, learn to draw a quirky, patchwork duck.

what you'll need

- Plain white paper
- Black fine-point marker

instructions

1 On white paper, draw the basic outline of a duck with a black fine-point marker. Ⓐ

2 Draw a beak and an eye on the duck, and doodle stripes around the neck and on the tail. Ⓑ

3 Create a patchwork look on the body of the duck by drawing two horizontal lines and four vertical lines. In the center of the patchwork, draw a swirly circle. In the four squares adjacent to the center one, draw a large plus sign. Ⓒ

4 Create the look of water by doodling little semicircle waves surrounding the duck.

5 On a separate sheet of white paper, use the black marker to doodle a sign that says "Classic Duck."

tip

Use your imagination to fill in the patchwork on the body of the duck. Feature a different shape in each square, or fill the squares with dots or stripes.

Ⓐ

Ⓑ

Ⓒ

BIG FISH, Little Fish

DOODLE PROMPT: Doodle a whole school of unique fish by giving each one its own pattern.

try it

On white paper, draw two large fish outlines, one medium fish outline, and two small fish outlines with a black fine-point marker. Draw two fins on each fish, and add stripes to all of the fins. Doodle scallops on each fish tail. Draw a small mouth and an eye on each fish. Doodle a pattern on each body, using stripes, dashes, dots, or a patchwork. Doodle bubbles coming out of each fish's mouth. On a separate piece of paper, doodle a sign in block letters that reads "Big Fish, Little Fish."

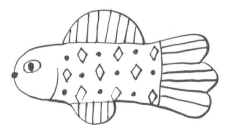

VIRTUOSO Violin

DOODLE PROMPT: Learn to doodle a violin in just a few simple steps.

try it

With a pencil on a white piece of paper, doodle the main shape of a violin, which is basically a large oval with a few curled notches on the side. Draw a parallel line on the top and right-hand side of the violin to give it dimension. Draw the tailpiece, the bridge, the fingerboard, and the scroll. Then draw four vertical lines for strings, from the scroll to the tailpiece. Doodle the F holes (shaped like an S and a mirror image of S) on each side of the strings. Retrace the pencil lines with a black fine-point marker, let dry, and then erase the pencil marks. On a separate piece of paper, create a coordinating sign that reads "violin" in elegant block letters.

Monika Forsberg

BOLD Eagle

DOODLE PROMPT: Bold lines make this eagle a force to be reckoned with.

what you'll need

- Plain white paper
- Black fine-point marker

instructions

1 On white paper, draw the basic outline of an eagle with a black fine-point marker. **Ⓐ**

2 Draw lines for the torso of the eagle, and doodle eyes and a beak.

3 Doodle large scallops along the whole top edge of the outspread wings, and smaller scallops to indicate the neck. **Ⓑ**

4 For the look of feathers, draw slightly irregular lines coming down from the wing scallops to the bottom edge of the wings.

5 Doodle stripes on the tail, and draw feather marks on the body. **Ⓒ**

6 On a separate piece of white paper, write out "Eagle" in block letters and then doodle dashed lines coming out of the top.

tip

Try adding color to your eagle to make the bold lines really pop.

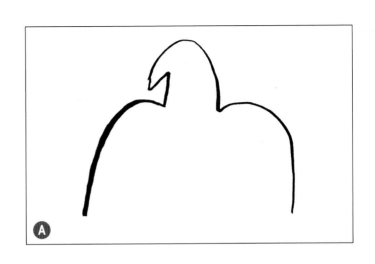

PRESSED and TRACED Flowers

DOODLE PROMPT: These artistic doodles begin as simple outlines of flowers and leaves, handpicked in your own backyard and then pressed in a book.

what you'll need

- Flowers and leaves
- Old newspaper
- Big, heavy books
- Washi tape
- White heavyweight paper
- Black fine-point marker
- Permanent markers in assorted colors

instructions

1 Gather various flowers and leaves, and carefully flatten each specimen inside a piece of folded newspaper. Slip each wrapped item within the pages of a heavy book, close the book, and stack another heavy book or two on top. Wait at least two weeks, then check to see if the collected plant parts are fully pressed and dry. **Ⓐ**

2 Remove your pressed plants from the newspaper, and arrange them on heavyweight paper in a pleasing design. Use a few small strips of washi tape to secure them in place. **Ⓑ**

3 Trace around the flowers and leaves twice with a black fine-point marker, so the outlines consist of two fine black lines. **Ⓒ**

4 Remove the washi tape and pressed plants from the paper.

5 Inside the outlines, doodle such details as curly lines, polka dots, scallops, and triangles.

6 Use permanent markers to add color to your drawing. **Ⓓ**

Ⓐ

Ⓑ

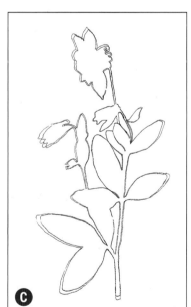

Ⓒ

Ⓓ

tips

- Use colored paper as the base for an interesting take on the flowers and leaves.
- For a different look, try drawing the flower and leaves freehand rather than tracing them.

Julia Grimm

FANTASY Land Maps

DOODLE PROMPT: Creatively use random watercolor marks as a base for drawing imaginary maps.

what you'll need

- Plain white paper
- Small paintbrush
- Watercolors
- Sea salt
- Black fine-point marker

instructions

1 Randomly add various colors to a piece of white paper using a small paintbrush and watercolors. Use a lot of water with the watercolors so they spread on the page easily. Leave some white space on the page amidst the color. **Ⓐ**

2 Before the ink dries, sprinkle some sea salt on the watercolors to create a unique effect.

3 Once the watercolors dry, trace the outer edge of the colored areas with a black fine-point marker. **Ⓑ**

4 Add doodled map elements, such as partial triangles for mountains, dots for trail markers, trees, boats, small buildings, and banners and words for the place names. **Ⓒ**

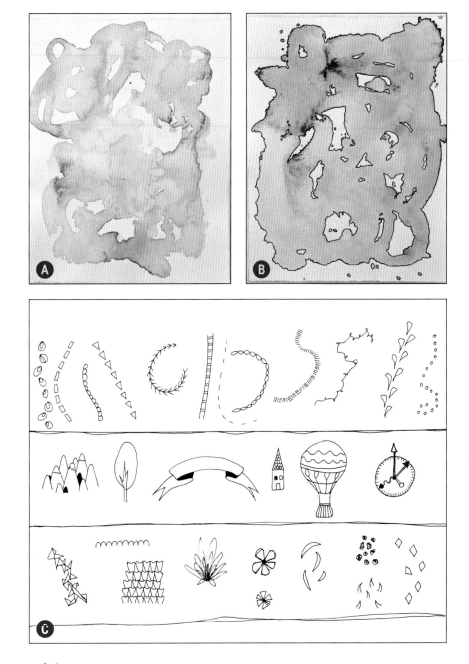

tips

- The sky is the limit with these imaginary maps. Try painting with watercolors on a piece of colored paper for an immediately different effect, or vary the specific colors of paints you use even more for an even wilder look.
- Try approaching this exercise with a slightly different medium— acrylic paint, for example. How might the map look with a different substrate as the base?

Julia Grimm

Time for TEA

DOODLE PROMPT: Play with overlapping doodles to create this fun abstract art.

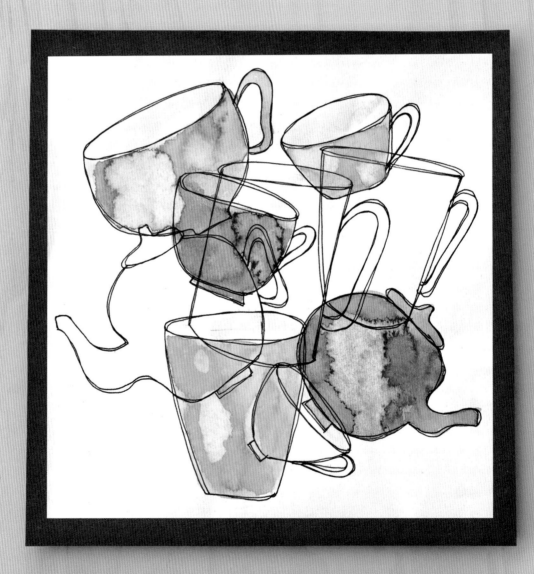

what you'll need

- Plain white paper
- Black fine-point marker
- Small paintbrush
- Watercolors
- Small jar of water

instructions

1 Draw a simple teacup in the middle of a white piece of paper with a black fine-point marker. Trace around it a second and a third time so the outline is made up of three black lines.

2 In the same manner, create a second teacup beside the first one, allowing some edges to overlap.

3 Continue to add teacups, teapots, and mugs of various shapes and sizes, with each new doodle overlapping in some way. Turn your paper sideways or upside-down to draw at a new angle. Ⓐ

4 Use watercolors and a small paintbrush to add various colors and shades to some of the teacups. Ⓑ

tips

- Try approaching this same exercise with different subject matter. For instance, birds, articles of clothing, pieces of fruit, leaves, or faces would make a great doodled collage. You could even personalize a doodle to make special gifts for friends, based on their favorite hobbies.
- Add simple patterns such as hearts, polka dots, or stars to your teacups before adding color with watercolors.

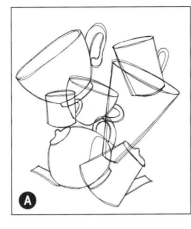

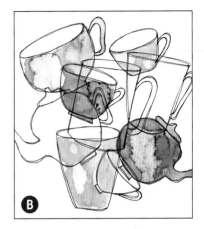

Julia Grimm

STYLISH Updo

DOODLE PROMPT: Design your own twisty hairdo with organic doodles and eye-catching colors.

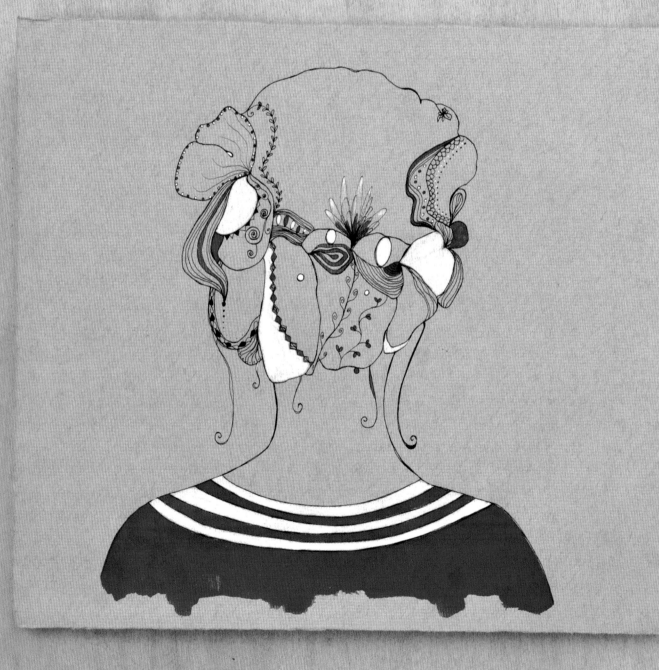

what you'll need

- Brown heavyweight paper
- Black fine-point marker
- Pencil (optional)
- Eraser (optional)
- Red colored marker
- White colored pencil

instructions

1 On brown heavyweight paper, draw the back of a figure's neck and shoulders with a black fine-point marker.

2 Form the outline of an updo hairstyle by drawing several irregular circular shapes next to each other, to indicate knots and twists in the hair at the nape of the neck. Ⓐ

NOTE
If you are feeling cautious, draw the back of the head and hair doodles first in pencil, and then trace over the pencil marks with the marker. Once the ink is dry, erase the pencil marks. If you're feeling not-so-cautious, grab the marker and begin!

3 Doodle wavy lines, hearts, dots, diamonds, and scallops in various patterns within different segments of the hairstyle. Leave a few of the segments empty. Ⓑ

4 Fill in some of the doodles with color using a red colored marker. Fill in other sections with a white colored pencil. Ⓒ

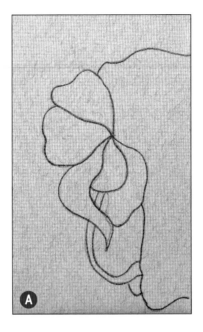

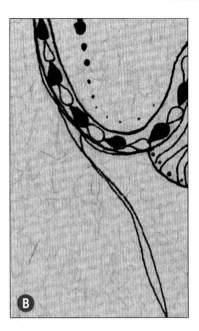

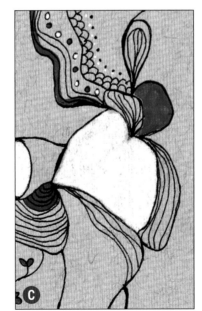

tips

- Research updos on the Internet, and doodle to imitate some of your favorite finds.
- Try all sorts of different hairstyles, from a pixie cut to a long ponytail.

51

Julia Grimm

Woodland Creature CARDS

DOODLE PROMPT: Make cheerful doodled animal cards with simple lines.

what you'll need

- Plain white paper
- Pencil
- Eraser
- Fine-point black marker
- Permanent markers in assorted colors
- Scissors
- Brown textured cardstock
- Glue stick

instructions

1 Use a pencil to doodle a set of woodland creatures on a piece of white paper. Focus on simple, organic shapes to create the major outlines of each animal. For the fox, start with a basic face shape Ⓐ. Add details to the face Ⓑ, then the body Ⓒ, and then the tail Ⓓ.

2 Doodle details, such as polka dots, flowers, and scallops, on some of the animals.

3 When you are satisfied with your drawings, go over all of the pencil marks with a black fine-point marker. Add two lines of black marker for every one line of pencil, so that each animal's outline is made up of two thin lines. Let the ink dry, and then erase the pencil marks. Ⓔ

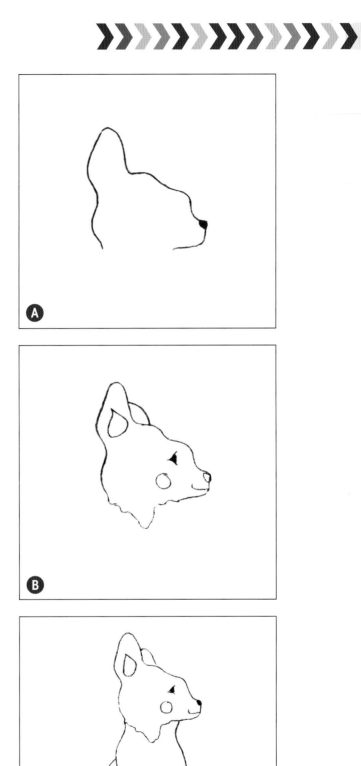

4 Doodle in a similar manner to make a bird Ⓕ, owl Ⓖ, raccoon Ⓗ, squirrel Ⓘ, and rabbit Ⓙ.

5 Add splashes of color to each woodland creature with permanent markers.

6 Cut an irregular oval around each woodland creature with a pair of scissors.

7 Doodle a border of wavy lines, dots, scallops, or diamonds around the edge of each oval with the black marker.

8 Use a glue stick to adhere each oval to a piece of brown textured cardstock, and then cut a larger brown oval around each white oval.

D

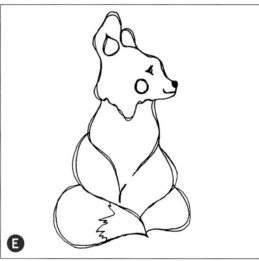

E

tip

- Adhere an animal card to a package as decoration.
- Make pairs of animal cards to use as a memory game for children.

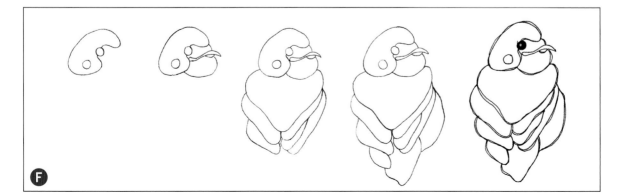

F

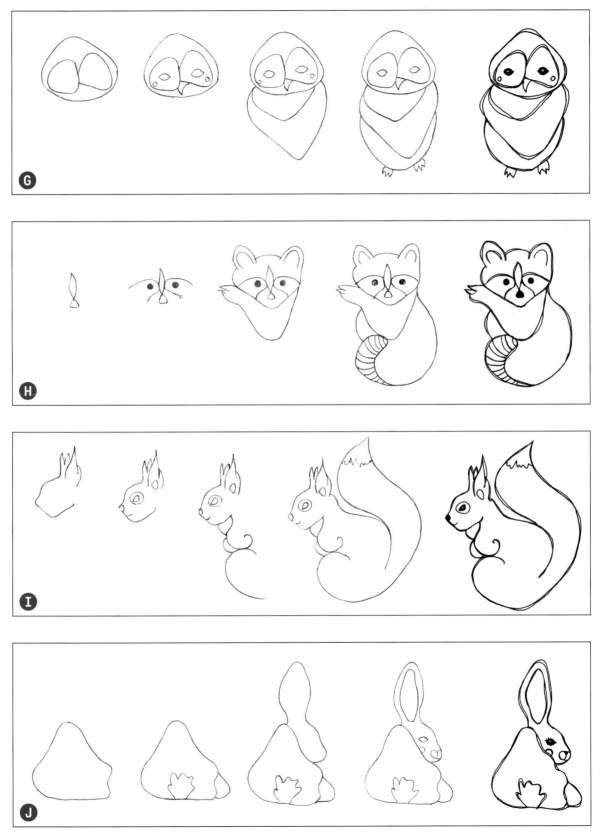

Build a BIRD

DOODLE PROMPT: This exercise presents all the pieces you need to doodle a complete bird, but it's up to you to choose just the right combination of features to your liking.

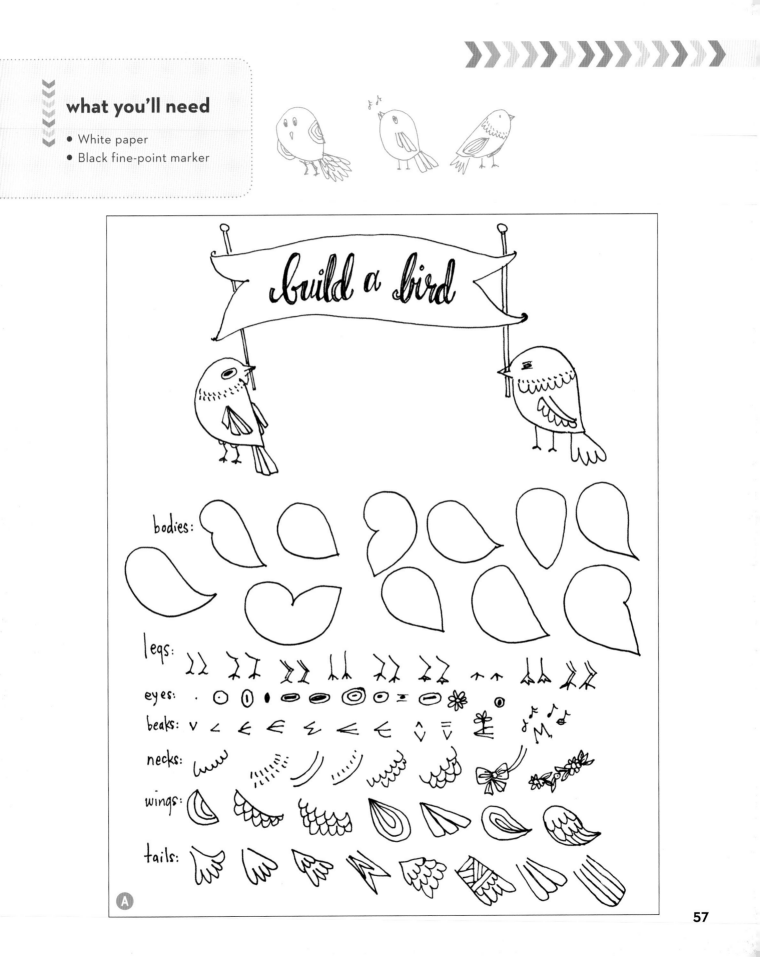

build a bird

bodies:

legs:

eyes:

beaks:

necks:

wings:

tails:

Ⓐ

instructions

1 Select a body shape from the collection of bird parts Ⓐ and draw it on a white piece of paper with a black fine-point marker. Ⓑ

2 Select a pair of legs and draw them coming from the bottom of the bird's body. Ⓒ

3 Select facial features, such as a beak and an eye, and draw them on the bird's head. Also select a neck treatment and draw that below the facial features. Ⓓ

4 Choose a coordinating wing and tail and draw them on your bird. Depending on the pose of your bird doodle, you may need to draw one or two eyes and one or two wings. Ⓔ

5 Doodle details on your bird that add personality, such as a flower or banner in its beak, or song notes coming from its mouth.

 tip
Try this same exercise with any variety of subject matter. When you break down a character or animal into their individual parts, they don't seem as daunting!

COLORFULLY INKED Flowers

DOODLE PROMPT: In this exercise, randomly placed ink splats become the base for beautiful flowers.

try it

On white pieces of cardstock, with watercolors and a small paintbrush, make large splashes of color that roughly resemble flower shapes. Let the shapes dry. To make the flowers more apparent, loosely outline the color shapes with a black extra-fine-point marker. Depending on the color splash, you may want to draw your flowers from the side or from the top. To finish, doodle individual leaves, petals, and details within each flower drawing.

DOODLED Letters

DOODLE PROMPT: Doodles do more than just look cute in this exercise. Here, they actually make up the letters that tell the story!

what you'll need

- Black cardstock
- Pencil
- White gel pen
- Eraser

instructions

1 On a black piece of cardstock, lightly sketch the letter A with a pencil. This will serve as a guide throughout the project.

2 With a white gel pen, draw two or three short lines next to each other at various points along the sketched A. Ⓐ

3 Doodle flowers of various sizes and shapes to fill in the spaces between the groups of lines. Let the ink dry.

4 Lightly erase the original pencil markings.

tip

The sky's the limit for approaching doodled letters. Use wavy or zigzag lines instead of straight ones, and use polka dots or stars instead of flowers, just to name a few variations.

Pam Garrison

PATCHWORK Doodles

DOODLE PROMPT: Create a colorful patchwork art
piece with just watercolors and a marker!

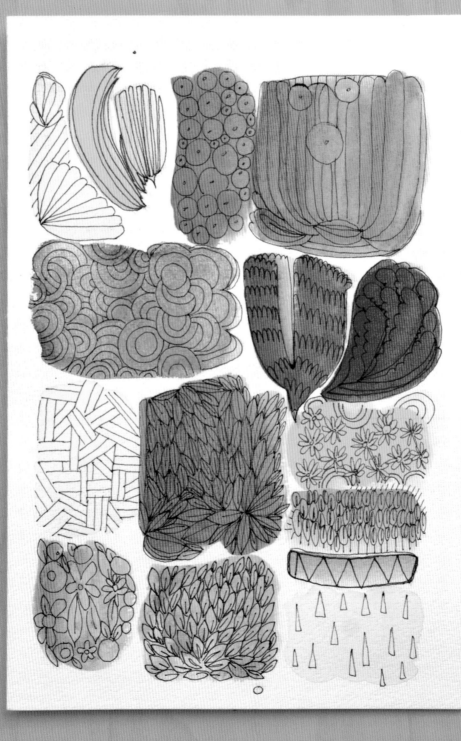

what you'll need

- White cardstock
- Watercolors in assorted colors
- Small paintbrush
- Small jar of water
- Black fine-point marker

instructions

1 On a piece of white cardstock, paint several patches of color using watercolors and a small paintbrush. Make sure to leave some white space in between each patch. Ⓐ

2 Let the paint dry completely.

3 Within each colored patch, doodle a different shape and pattern with a black fine-point marker. Keep your doodled lines within each color, and do not doodle out into the white area. Within each patch, use scallops, dots, feathers, triangles, flowers, leaves, and whatever else you'd like to doodle. You might even combine a few different patterns within one color, such as the concentric circles and the flowers in the yellow patch. Ⓑ

4 Outline some of the doodles completely with the black marker, as done with the brown patch with diamond shapes, the purple feathery patch, the yellow banana-shaped patch, and the pink scalloped patch. Ⓒ

tip

This exercise would be interesting to try with just one or two colors, or even with just black and white doodles and no watercolors.

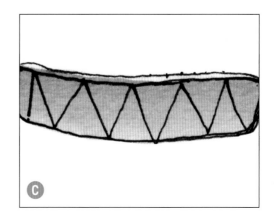

CELEBRATION Banner

DOODLE PROMPT: Banners are a fun and easy subject to draw. They make a great addition to another drawing or work as a standalone doodle.

banners

what you'll need

- Plain white paper
- Black fine-point marker

instructions

1 On white paper, draw two parallel, slightly curved lines with a black fine-point marker. Connect the ends with two more parallel lines Ⓐ. Repeat to make three curved rectangles stacked on top of one other, with some white space in between. Ⓑ

2 Just to the left of the top banner, draw the tail of an arrow shape, and connect it to the banner. Draw another arrow tail, facing the opposite direction, to the right of the bottom banner. Ⓒ

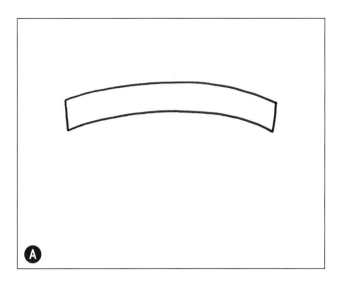

Ⓐ

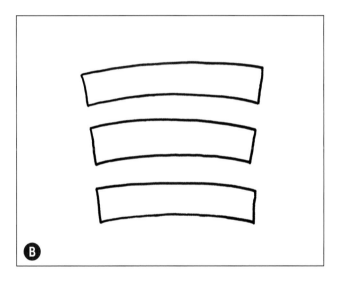

Ⓑ

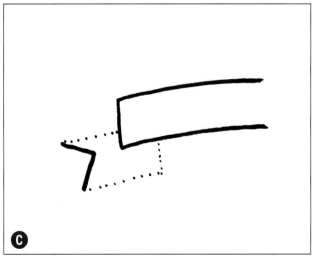

Ⓒ

3 Between the first and second rectangle, and again between the second and third rectangle, draw two parallel diagonal lines that connect the word rectangles. **Ⓓ**

4 Doodle shading stripes in the two arrow-shaped boxes and the two diagonal boxes. **Ⓔ**

5 Doodle a word in each of the three rectangles, varying the lettering style.

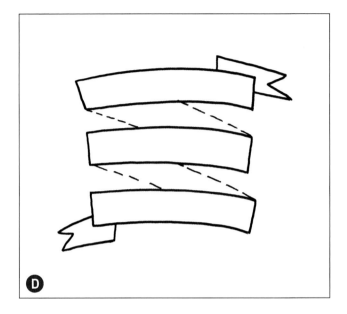

Ⓓ

Ⓔ

MAKE

FUN

banners

tips

- To add more dimension, fill in some of the banner to make it look like a shadow.
- Play with the ends of the banner by making the tails longer or curvier.

COUNTDOWN Calendar

DOODLE PROMPT: Learn to doodle a fun countdown calendar that is sure to increase excitement for any upcoming event.

try it

On a white piece of paper, doodle boxes of various sizes with a black fine-point marker. Make the boxes slightly different by giving some of them a double outline and some of them a shadow. Doodle the countdown numbers in fun fonts within each box. Doodle radiating dashes around the box with the 1 in it, to make it stand out. Doodle the words, "Only 10 Days To Go" (or the number of days of your countdown).

To use the countdown calendar, you could just draw a big X through the appropriate box each day. To make it more fun, consider using stickers, colored markers, or washi tape to mark each passing day.

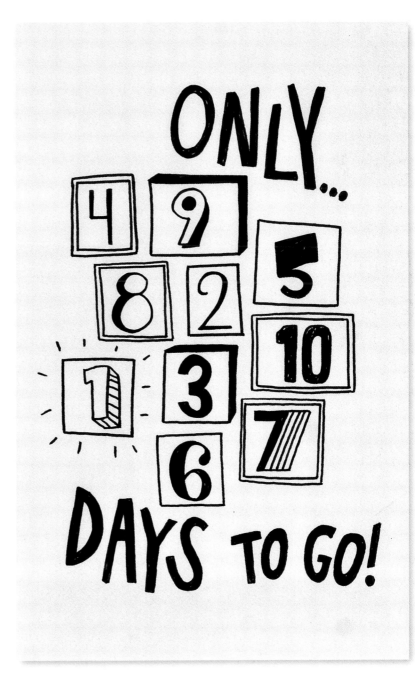

Kate Gabrielle

FLAPPER Doodle

DOODLE PROMPT: This simple cartoon character, with her jazz-age haircut and fun fringe dress, is loaded with personality.

what you'll need

- Plain white paper
- Black fine-point marker

instructions

1 Near the top of a white piece of paper, use a black fine-point marker to draw a circle for the head. (A)

2 Doodle hair across the head in the shape of a sideways C. Leave a white zigzag space open to make the hair look shiny. (B)

3 Draw two large U shapes for eyes and one small upside-down U shape for the nose. (C)

4 Draw a line for the mouth, with two tiny triangles above the line and one tiny square below the line. Fill in the mouth shapes with the marker.

5 Draw a neck coming down from the head. (D)

6 Doodle the flapper dress by making rows of wide zigzag patterns that grow in width with each row.

7 Doodle two arms, two legs, and two triangles for the shoes.

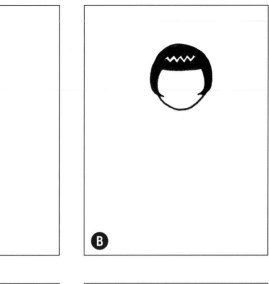

tips

- Experiment with a different hairstyle or a different outfit.
- Give the flapper girl an accessory or two, such as a fun hairpiece or a purse.

REAL LIFE Doodles

DOODLE PROMPT: Constantly inspired by everyday items, I like to challenge myself to create scenes using those simple items as the base. I place an item, such as a paperclip, a cracker, a piece of fruit, or a flower on a piece of paper and then I doodle a scene around that item. It's amazing what your eye can see when given the chance.

GRAPE Guy

After eating a cluster of grapes, the remaining stem looked like a tree to me so I treated it as such and doodled a boy leaning against the "tree."

A small cluster of grapes became balloons in the next doodle and a single grape became a single balloon flying away from the doodled boy.

TASTY Palette

A small handful of colored candies laid on a piece of paper made me think of paint colors, so I arranged them evenly and drew an artist's palette around them.

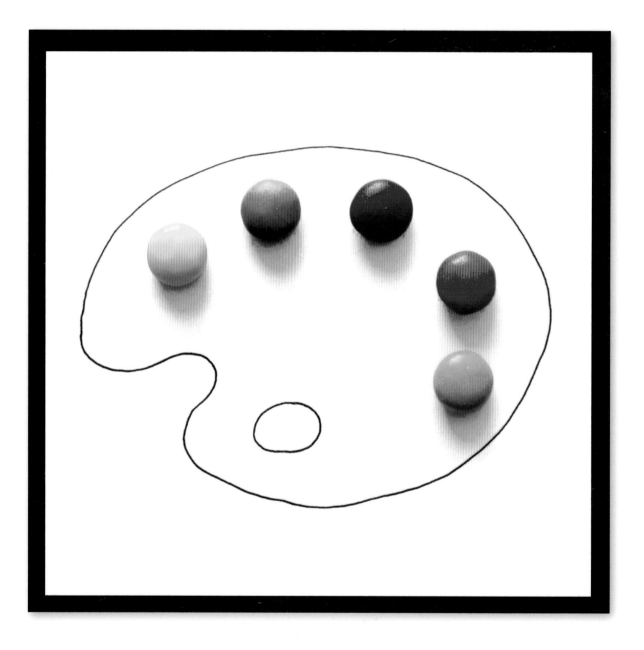

COOKIE Globe

A half-eaten cookie caught my eye when I noticed it vaguely resembled the continents on a globe. I simply added the stand and instantly had the world at my fingertips.

RECORD Player

A half-eaten cookie looked like a record to me so I made a simple doodle
of a turntable around the cookie to get the full effect.

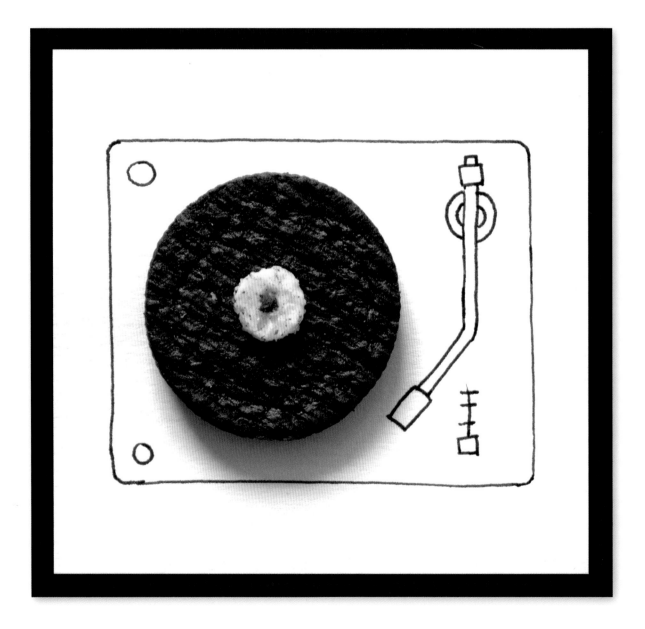

TRUSTY Trumpet

A paperclip became the main part of a trumpet in this drawing. I only needed to doodle a small mouthpiece, finger buttons, and the bell of the trumpet to make it complete.

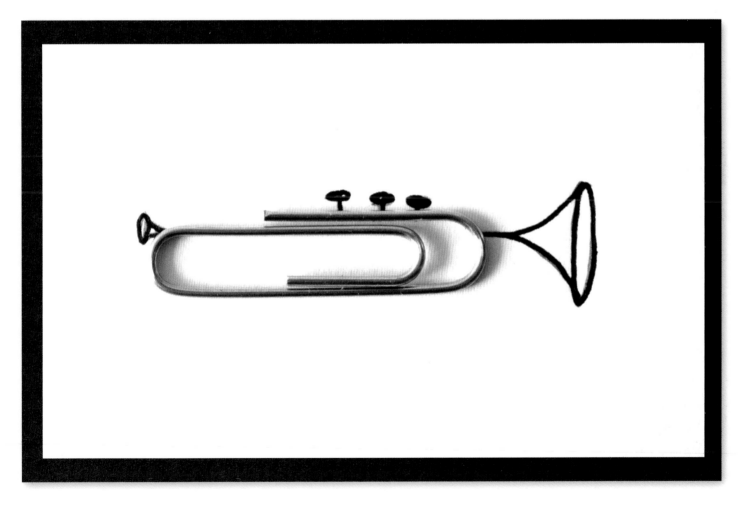

OOPSIE Doodle Birds

DOODLE PROMPT: I accidentally smeared a colored pigment stick on one of my journal pages. Initially I was frustrated because I don't like wasting paper with smudges or mistakes, but the longer I looked at the smear, the more I saw the shape of a little bird. I turned that "mistake" into the base of an entire party of bird friends!

what you'll need

- White cardstock
- Small paintbrush
- Small jar of water
- Pigment sticks in assorted colors
- Black fine-point marker

instructions

1 On a piece of white cardstock, create several teardrop shapes using a watered-down paintbrush and pigment sticks in assorted colors. Don't worry about making the teardrops perfectly symmetrical or even similar to each other. The more irregular the shape, the more personality each bird will have. Let the colors dry. Ⓐ

2 On each bird, doodle a small triangle with a line down the middle for a beak, a larger triangle for a party hat, and stick figure legs. Ⓑ

Ⓐ

Ⓑ

3 Doodle a petal shape for a wing and outline each teardrop bird, body shape with a black fine-point marker. Ⓒ

4 Doodle details to give each bird personality, such as polka dots, stripes, zigzag lines, or scallops. Ⓓ

5 Add splashes of color to each bird's party hat using the pigment sticks and the small paintbrush.

6 Doodle the words "Party Time!" on the bottom of the cardstock with the black marker, and fill in the space on the P, A, and R (page 76).

tip

Use this same basic method to really stretch your imagination. See a smudge on a piece of paper? Use your imagination to "see" a shape in that smudge, and create something beautiful from it.

Ⓒ

Ⓓ

DREAMY Doodled Garden

DOODLE PROMPT: Doodle a garden full of flowers. No green thumb needed!

⟫ try it

On a piece of white paper, doodle a variety of flower heads with a black fine-point marker. Doodle the heads of tulips, daisies, and other flowers you might actually see in a flower garden, but also doodle rounded triangles and big circles for flowers from your imagination. Add details to the flower heads using zigzag lines, dots, and stripes. Draw stems from the base of each flower head, and doodle the ground where all the stems meet. Doodle leaves and grass, and then fill in parts of the leaves and flowers with the black marker.

FRAMED Words

DOODLE PROMPT: Funky doodled frames surround special quotes and meaningful phrases.

⌄ try it

Draw a large, irregular, double-lined oval with a black fine-point marker on white paper. Add petals around the oval by doodling semi-circles one row at a time. Add details to the petals by drawing curved lines within each one. Doodle "Make it count" or a favorite phrase inside the main oval, filling in parts of the letters with the marker. Add color to the background using a pink permanent marker.

This exercise can be interpreted and played with in so many different ways. Start with a different base shape, choose a different accent shape or different details, or add color in unique ways to make different parts of the doodle pop.

The Girl with
DOODLED HAIR

DOODLE PROMPT: At first glance, this doodled girl may look complicated to create. But broken down into individual doodles, she's a piece of cake—and as sweet as can be.

what you'll need

- White cardstock
- Black fine-point marker

instructions

1 Start this doodle on the left side of a piece of white cardstock by drawing one small leaf with a black fine-point marker. (A)

2 Stemming out from this one leaf, doodle various leaf and petal shapes that all build on each other. Vary the style and direction of each petal and leaf shape as you go. (B)

A

B

3 Slowly wind the entire section up and down to form a large irregular U shape. Ⓒ

4 Doodle the girl's face, neck, and upper body coming down from the hair shape. Add eyes, a nose, a mouth, and freckles. Ⓓ

5 Add details throughout the hair by filling in each petal and leaf shape with swirls and lines.

tip

This doodle girl can have all sorts of crazy hairstyles—whatever you can dream up! Try doodling a girl with hair made up of triangles or circles. Or, stick with the petal shape but, for a new look, feature different doodled details such as dashes or polka dots within each shape.

designer: THEO ELLSWORTH

Doodle RIDER

DOODLE PROMPT: A simple figure and a set of wheels become the ultimate doodle rider in this fun exercise.

what you'll need

- White cardstock
- Black fine-point marker

instructions

1 On a piece of white cardstock, draw two circles with a black fine-point marker.

2 Doodle the outline of a sitting figure between and slightly higher than the two circles. Ⓐ

3 Doodle the outline of a vehicle by bringing the rider and the wheels together with lines. Ⓑ

4 Draw lines within the outlined figure and vehicle to match the shape. For example, draw circular lines within the tires and vertical lines across the figure's shirt and vehicle.

5 Cover the figure's head by doodling small lines across the entire shape.

6 Doodle several horizontal lines below and behind the vehicle to represent a road. Ⓒ

tip

Don't worry about making sure that the doodle makes visual sense. Just have fun!

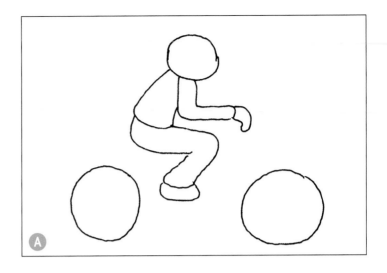

Never-Before-Seen CHARACTER

DOODLE PROMPT: Begin this exercise by—wait for it—closing your eyes! Doodle without looking, and then transform your unique doodle into a brand-new character.

❯ try it

Select a white piece of paper and a black fine-point marker. Put your marker to the paper, close your eyes, and doodle a small design without looking and without lifting the marker. Open your eyes and take a look at the doodle. Can you see a face in the doodle? Add eyes, a mouth, ears, hair, and a nose to make the shape look even more like a face. Draw a loose rectangle beneath the head for a torso. Add legs and shoes, arms and hands, and a few details to indicate clothing.

ANIMAL Friend

DOODLE PROMPT: Doodle a friendly, quirky animal by starting with a basic outline and then jazzing it up one line at a time.

try it

Draw the outline of an animal with a black fine-point marker on white paper. There's no need to make the animal shape realistic; instead, keep it simple, and don't over-think what you're drawing. Doodle basic features on the animal, including a tail, hooves, eyes, and a mouth. Doodle lines around each feature so that the eye has several circles around it and so on. Continue adding straight and zigzag lines until the animal shape is filled.

GEO House

DOODLE PROMPT: Doodle a complex architectural shape by connecting simple geometric shapes with lines.

what you'll need

- White cardstock
- Black fine-point marker

instructions

1 On white paper, doodle several different geometric shapes in varying sizes with a black fine-point marker. (A)

2 Connect the shapes by drawing straight lines between them. (B)

3 Doodle straight and circular lines within the connector lines and geometric shapes. (C)

4 Doodle a simple character to the side of the structure, with a head, eyes, torso, arms, and legs. Draw lines at his wrists, ankles, waist, and neck to indicate clothing, and doodle a weird hat for him to wear.

5 Doodle a rough horizontal line in the background, with a few peaks to indicate the ground.

tip

Consider limiting yourself to just one shape or just one type of line to complete this exercise. Constraints have a way of prompting surprising solutions from your imagination.

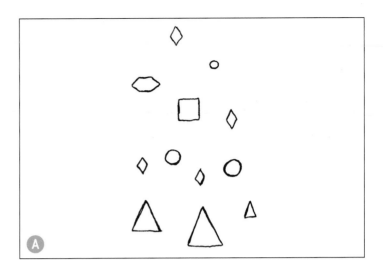

A

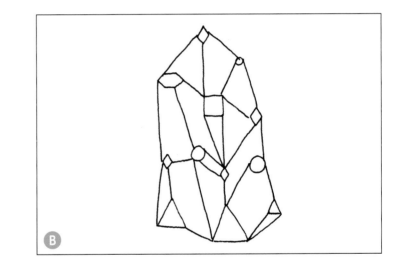

B

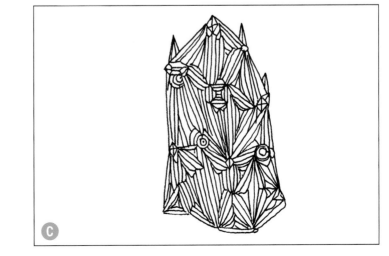

C

Manic for MONSTERS

DOODLE PROMPT: With only a black marker, doodle bold and unique monster faces.

try it

On white paper, doodle several sets of eyeballs with a black fine-point marker, starting with two larger circles next to each other and two smaller circles within each larger circle. Doodle organic, wavy head shapes around each set of eyeballs. Doodle mouths, noses, and ears on each monster head. Fill in the empty space on each monster face with repetitive doodles, such as straight lines, wavy lines, or scallops.

WILBUR the Dog

DOODLE PROMPT: Learn how to draw my scruffy dog Wilbur, complete with a scarf and a flower for accessories. If we were doodling something more realistic, Wilbur would more likely be carting a sandwich and food wrappers. He loves to steal my lunch!

what you'll need

- Plain white paper
- Black markers in assorted thicknesses

instructions

1 On white paper, use a black fine-point marker to doodle the main outline of a puppy, using scribbles and squiggly lines. Ⓐ

2 Loosely retrace over the squiggly lines for added texture, and continue with those lines to fill in the dog's ears. Draw and fill in three circles for the two eyes and nose. Ⓑ

C

3 Doodle a triangle for the front part of the puppy's scarf and two irregular rectangles for the ends of the scarf. Fill the scarf in with dots, line, and dashes. Add tassels to the bottom of the scarf. **C**

4 Doodle a striped flower as if the dog is holding it in its mouth.

5 Retrace the puppy outline a third time with a thicker black marker. **D**

tip

Throughout this entire exercise, keep your hand loose, and don't press down too hard with the pen. This will help achieve that loose, fur-like doodle.

D

EMBROIDERED Mittens

DOODLE PROMPT:
The basic shape of a
mitten is pretty simple,
which means there's
even more time to
focus on doodling the
embroidery work.

 try it

On white paper, draw a large
outline of a mitten with a black
fine-point marker. Doodle
a border around the entire
mitten, made up of solid lines,
dashes, or scallops. Doodle
an embroidery pattern down
the center of the mitten, using
groups of flowers, circles, cross
stitches, or other shapes.

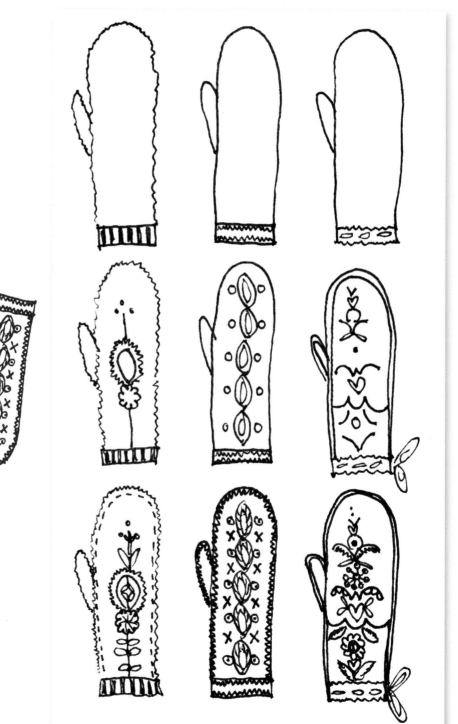

TEA Time

DOODLE PROMPT:
Learn to draw the fanciest of teacups!

⟩ try it

On white paper, use a black fine-point marker to doodle the main outline of a teacup. Draw a plate around the bottom of the teacup. Doodle polka dots, scallops, and stripes on the top and bottom of the plate. Add rows of doodles to the teacup using small flowers, scallops, stripes, and polka dots. The more you can fit on this tiny cup, the better! Finish by drawing tiny dots and stripes wherever they will fit among the patterns.

Lindsay Mason

CHEERFUL
Song Bird

DOODLE PROMPT: Doodling designs on this friendly bird means you can give her any kind of personality you'd like!

what you'll need

- Plain white paper
- Black fine-point marker

instructions

1 On white paper, use a black fine-point marker to draw a circle for the bird's head and a large teardrop shape for the bird's body. Draw a wing shape over the body. Add the bird's tail, legs, and beak. Ⓐ

2 Doodle the head feathers, and draw the eye, eyelashes, and a cheek on the bird's head. Add lines to the inside shape of the wing and tail. Ⓑ

97

3 Fill in the body with sections of doodles, such as scallops, ovals, and dashes. Add more detail lines to the tail and wing. Doodle three lines coming out of the tail feathers with dots on the tips. **C**

4 Add tiny dots around the entire outline of the bird, plus a few coming out of the tail feathers and head feathers. Fill in some of the stripes of the wing. **D**

tip

Play around with various patterns on and around the bird's body and tail. You could even make a whole bird family, all with different patterns!

FRIENDLY Fashionista

DOODLE PROMPT: Take this cartoon girl's fashion sense over the top with a completely customized, doodled look.

what you'll need

- Plain white paper
- Black fine-point marker

instructions

1 On white paper, draw the outline of a girl's body with a black fine-point marker. Try starting with the jaw line, then move down the neck, shoulders, arms, and finally the skirt and legs. Then go back up and finish around the top of the head. **Ⓐ**

2 Doodle the basic outlines of a shirt, skirt, shoes, hair, and a hat.

3 Doodle details on the clothing, such as stripes on the shoes, ruching around the waist, a leaf pattern on the hat, and a variety of doodled patterns on the skirt. **Ⓑ**

4 Doodle a big flower on the side of the girl's hat. Draw two small wavy lines for the eyes and eyelashes, and draw a small mouth.

5 Add additional details to the clothing and shading to the legs with very light dash marks. **Ⓒ**

tip

Once you've doodled the basic outline of a girl, anything goes for the clothing. Try doodling a dress or pants or adding more accessories.

Ⓐ

FLOWER Boat

DOODLE PROMPT: Who said doodles have to be realistic? Playing with scenes that are purely for fun lets the mind wander rather than worry about perfecting the details. Add in a scrap piece of wood and some bright paints, and you've got the perfect recipe for a carefree, artistic afternoon.

what you'll need

- Scrap piece of wood
- Black fine-point marker
- Acrylic paint in assorted colors
- Small paintbrush
- Small jar of water as needed

instructions

1 With a black fine-point marker on a scrap piece of wood, doodle a row of waves.

2 Draw the shape of a boat on the water with one horizontal line and two rounded sides. (A)

3 Doodle flowers with curvy stems and leaves coming out of the boat. (B) and (C)

4 With acrylic paint and a small paintbrush, paint the flowers pink with yellow centers, the leaves green, and the background blue. Leave the boat unpainted so it's the color of the wood.

5 Once the paint has dried, go over all of the outlines with the black marker. (D)

tip

Experiment with different flower varieties, sizes, and colors.

(A)

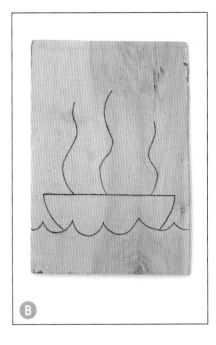
(B)

(C)

(D)

BAD LUCK Skull

DOODLE PROMPT: In this doodle, words are just as important as the shapes.

⟩⟩ try it

Doodle a skull with a black fine-point marker on white paper. Thicken the outline by going over it a few times with the marker. Write the letters B and D where the eyes should be, and the letter A where the nose should be. Doodle a smile for the skull with one curved line and several vertical lines. Doodle a pipe coming out of the skull's mouth with a large cloud of smoke above it. Within the cloud, doodle the letters L, U, C, and K.

The basic shapes of this doodle are the perfect canvas to play with word choices. Think of three letter-words to make up the skull's facial features and a corresponding word to put in the cloud.

MOON Man

DOODLE PROMPT: This crescent moon has a flower for an eye and personality to boot.

try it

Doodle the outline of a crescent moon with a black fine-point marker on white paper, making a small triangle shape for a nose on the inner curve. Thicken the moon outline by going over it a few times with the marker. Draw a circle to the right of the nose, and doodle petals around it for the flower eye. Draw a curved line beneath the nose, and doodle egg-shaped teeth along the length of the line. Doodle several raindrop shapes, and fill some of them in with the black marker.

TRANSPARENT
Doodling

DOODLE PROMPT: I'm constantly gathering photos, patterned paper, cards, magazine prints, and various other items that inspire me. In one of my favorite doodling exercises, I combine a group of favorite items in one drawing on a piece of transparent plastic. No need to use expensive transparent paper—plastic or cellophane bags work just as well.

what you'll need

- Photos, magazine clippings, patterned paper, or anything else that inspires you and is traceable
- Masking tape
- Transparent paper, a piece of cellophane, or a plastic bag
- Black permanent markers in assorted thicknesses
- Heavy eraser (optional)

instructions

1 Choose one motif from your inspirational clippings that you want to be the focus of your drawing. Ⓐ

2 Use masking tape to attach the clipping to the back of a piece of transparent plastic, so the plastic is on top.

3 Trace the motif on the plastic with a black fine-point permanent marker. If you make a mistake as you're tracing, you can usually remove the marker from the plastic with a heavy eraser. Ⓑ

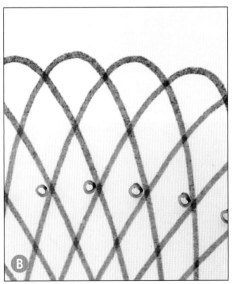

4 Remove the clipping from the plastic, and then adhere a new clipping to the plastic slightly to the side of the first drawing.

5 Trace the second motif onto the plastic with the same fine-point marker, but only trace the parts that don't interfere with the first motif, so it appears as if the second motif is behind the first. **C**

6 Continue in this manner until you are satisfied with the amount of motifs combined for the drawing.

7 Outline the main shapes of each motif with a thicker black permanent marker. **D**

tip

This exercise doesn't have to stop with the transparent plastic. Instead, trace the entire image from the plastic onto a piece of white paper. Then doodle additional details, fill in the background, or add splashes of color.

CIRCLE COLLECTION

DOODLE PROMPT: Using only a black marker, draw bold circles filled with doodled details.

try it

On a piece of white paper, use a pencil to draw several circles and ovals of varying sizes, overlapping them as you go. Doodle small circles inside of larger circles, and draw little groups of circles that flow away from the main image. Trace over the pencil lines with thick and fine-point markers. Doodle details within the circles, such as stripes, polka dots, and scallops, and then add a few doodled details on the edges of the paper.

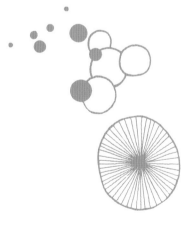

Heidi Vandal

DECORATIVE Owl

DOODLE PROMPT: A true-to-life image of an owl provides the base of this exercise, but some tracing and doodling makes this owl all your own.

what you'll need

- Owl image
- Transparent plastic
- Masking tape
- Black permanent markers in assorted thicknesses
- Plain white paper

instructions

1 Secure an owl image to the back of a piece of transparent plastic with masking tape.

2 Trace the owl onto the plastic with a black fine-point permanent marker. **Ⓐ**

3 Remove the owl image from the plastic. **Ⓑ**

Ⓐ

Ⓑ

4 Trace the owl from the plastic onto a piece of white paper with a black fine-point permanent marker. Retrace the main outlines of the body, feathers, and facial features with a thick black permanent marker. Ⓒ

5 Doodle details on the owl, such as dashed lines, arches, and scallops on the feathers, followed by dots, scallops, and petals on the face. Ⓓ

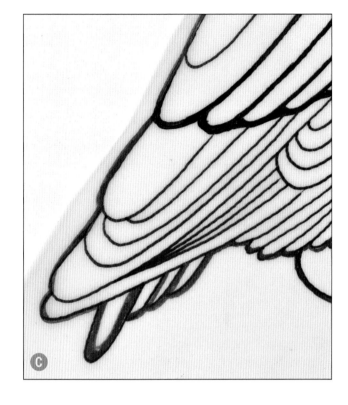

tip

Trace any shape or image with ease, and then let your creativity loose when you doodle within the shape. This approach provides a lot of freedom because it takes away the pressure of getting a main shape or character just right.

MANDALA

DOODLE PROMPT: A mandala is a great way to experiment with doodles, shapes, and symmetry.

what you'll need

- Plain white paper
- Compass
- Sharp pencil
- Black fine-point marker
- Eraser

instructions

1 On a piece of white paper, draw a large circle using a compass with a sharp pencil.

2 Divide the circle into 16 equal wedges by using the compass and pencil to draw light lines.

3 Using a black fine-point marker, doodle three small circles, each one bigger than the last, in the exact center of the large circle.

4 Continuing with the marker for the remaining steps, doodle two rows of arches around the circles, using the pencil lines as a guide to ensure symmetry throughout.

5 Doodle a row of petals around the arches. Ⓐ

6 Alternate between arches and petals until the entire circle is filled. Draw each layer bigger than the one before it, and don't worry about the details yet—just focus on the larger petals and arches. Ⓑ

Ⓐ

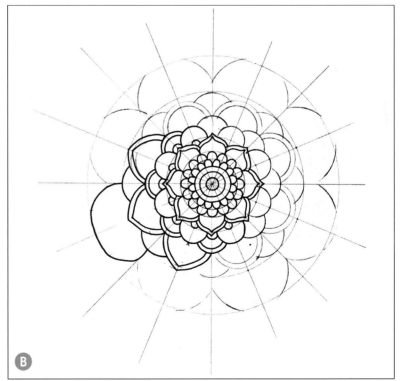

Ⓑ

C

7 Doodle details within the arches and petals. Add lines, scallops, stripes, smaller petals, thicker lines, and shading, keeping everything symmetrical according to the pencil guidelines. **©**

8 Let the ink dry completely, and then erase the pencil marks.

tips

- Make this exercise your own by playing with different shapes and doodled details. A mandala made up only of arches or of petals would be really fun to play with.
- Draw a mandala in black, and then draw the exact same mandala with colored markers. The difference might surprise you!

CUTE Kokeshi

DOODLE PROMPT: The more you look at your surroundings and notice details that others miss, the more addicting it will become! You'll want to carry your camera with you at all times to capture inspiration for your next doodled character.

what you'll need

- Heavyweight white paper
- Black fine-point marker
- Small paintbrush
- Watercolors
- Small jar of water

instructions

1 On heavyweight white paper, use a black fine-point marker to draw a rounded triangle shape for the outline of your kokeshi. Ⓐ

2 Block out the main pieces of the doll by drawing lines for the front fold of the kimono, the kimono sleeves, and the hairline. Ⓑ

3 Draw three open semicircles for the eyes and the nose, and draw rounded hands at the end of the kimono sleeves. Ⓒ

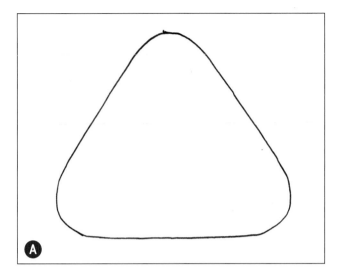

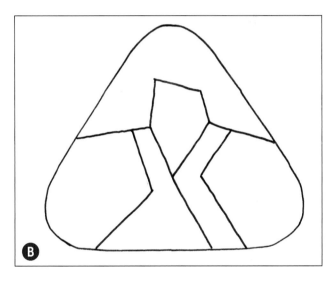

4 Doodle various patterns on the different parts of the kimono using flowers, stars, and lines. Ⓓ

5 Draw slightly wavy lines for the strands of hair. Ⓔ

6 Add color to the kokeshi with a small paintbrush and watercolors. Ⓕ

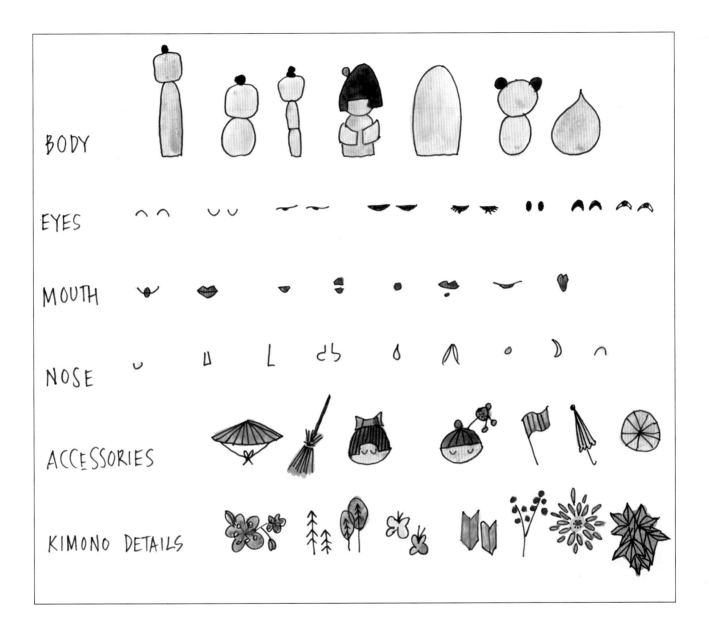

BODY

EYES

MOUTH

NOSE

ACCESSORIES

KIMONO DETAILS

tips

- With such a simple beginning shape, kokeshi are easily customized. Experiment with various patterns for the kimono, and maybe even add a few accessories such as scarves, umbrellas, or hair flowers.
- Instead of starting with a rounded triangle outline, experiment with other shapes, such as a cylinder, egg shape, or large circle.

Jan Avellana

SHAPELY Sun

DOODLE PROMPT: Geometric patterns fill this bright sunshine doodle.

what you'll need

- Black fine-point marker
- Heavyweight white paper
- Watercolors
- Watercolor brush
- Small jar of water

instructions

1 Draw a large circle with a black fine-point marker on heavyweight white paper.

2 For the sun rays, doodle alternating large and small triangles around the entire circle. Ⓐ

3 Draw evenly spaced rows within the circle.

4 Fill in each row with a zigzag pattern to create rows of alternating triangles. Ⓑ

5 Draw horizontal stripes within all the triangles that point downward and vertical stripes within all the triangles that point upward. Ⓒ

6 Add a deep golden color to the entire sun shape with watercolors.

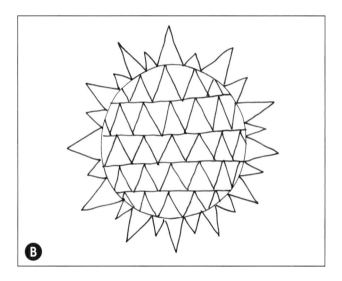

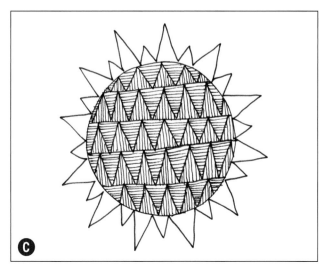

WHIRLWIND
Windmill

DOODLE PROMPT: Learn to doodle a whimsical Dutch windmill that's perfect for coloring in.

what you'll need

- Plain white paper
- Black fine-point marker
- Roll of masking tape
- Watercolor pencils in assorted colors
- Small jar of water

instructions

1 On white paper, trace the inside circle of a roll of masking tape with a black fine-point marker. Draw a smaller circle and a dot in the middle of the traced circle.

2 Draw the sides and base of the windmill. **Ⓐ**

3 Draw the blades of the windmill by making a large X through the center of the dotted circle. Doodle blade shapes at the end of each leg of the X.

4 Draw three vertical lines and three horizontal lines through the top circle of the windmill.

5 Doodle a decorative door. **Ⓑ**

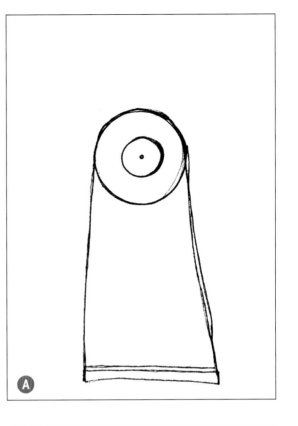

Ⓐ

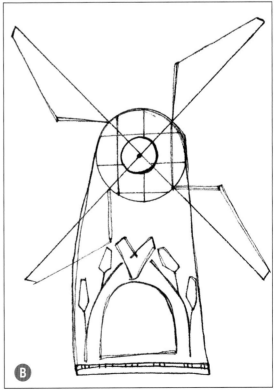

Ⓑ

6 Retrace all the lines you've drawn to make them stand out more, and add shading to the tiled part of the windmill. Ⓒ

7 Add splashes of color by wetting watercolor pencils and coloring in certain sections.

tips

- Change the color and style of your windmill to really make it your own!
- Add scenery, such as flowers, shrubbery, and rocks to the doodle for added interest.

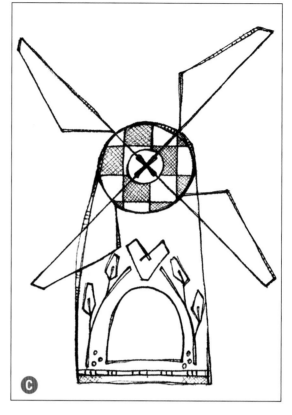

Ⓒ

Shades of STRAWBERRY

DOODLE PROMPT: Sample paint chips from the hardware store serve as the perfect substrate for these charming strawberry doodles.

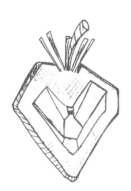

try it

Choose paint chips in various shades of pink. Doodle the outline of a strawberry on each one with a black fine-point marker. Doodle details within each strawberry to create different views of the strawberry. Doodle an angular heart on the middle of one of the strawberries and a stem and leaves on both. Add polka dots with a white gel pen on the second strawberry. Add a touch of color on both strawberries with colored pencils.

HOME Is Where the HEART Is

DOODLE PROMPT: Doodle a house inspired by pictures of houses you like, enhanced by your own imagination.

try it

On white paper, use a black fine-point marker to draw the basic outline of a house. Add doors, windows, scallops for the roof, and a heart-shaped weather vane. Use diagonal stripes to draw shading in the door and window frames. Add splashes of assorted color with colored pencils or watercolors.

Boats Among FLOWERS

DOODLE PROMPT: Simple geometric shapes (just lines and triangles!) become complex, interesting objects in this scene with lotus flowers and a paper boat. Try out new composition possibilities by using a square sheet of paper.

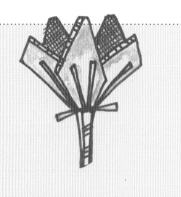

what you'll need

- White heavyweight paper
- Black fine-point marker
- Assorted colored pencils

instructions

1 In the lower right corner of a white piece of paper, use a black fine-point marker to draw triangles for the base of the boat. Add a narrow pyramid with a square on top to complete the boat. **Ⓐ**

2 Doodle three lotus flowers to the left of the boat, with diamond shapes and triangles for the flower heads and long skinny rectangles for each stem. Draw leaves on each flower, and add texture to the stems with stripes. **Ⓑ**

3 Doodle V shapes at the base of the flower stems.

4 Add stripes and crosshatching to the various shapes to give them depth. **Ⓒ**

5 Add splashes of colors with colored pencils.

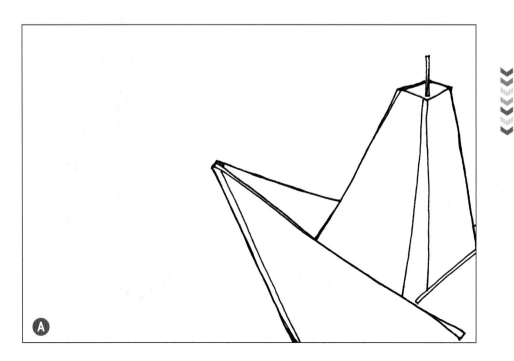

Ⓐ

tip

If you're having trouble visualizing the paper boat, find a tutorial online for how to fold a paper boat, and use that as a reference.

128

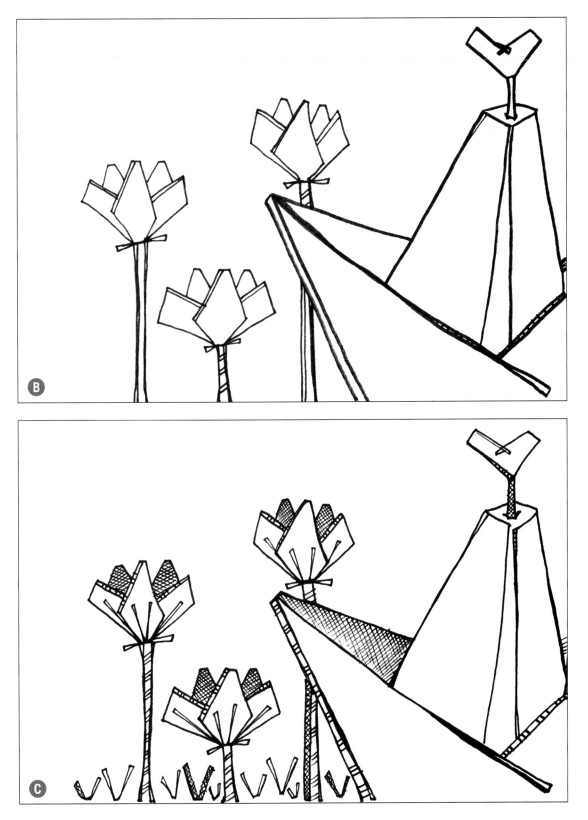

WOODLAND Girl

DOODLE PROMPT: There's no rule that says doodles have to be realistic. Sometimes it's more fun when they're not! This woodland girl, with her sweet cheeks and quirky antlers, exudes personality. You might doodle a whole forest of woodland creatures before you know it!

what you'll need

- Plain white paper
- Black fine-point marker
- Assorted colored pencils

instructions

1 On white paper, draw a round nose with a black fine-point marker. Draw two arches above the nose for eyebrows, and then draw angular cheekbones and a jaw line. Add a neck and shoulders, and doodle a small mouth. Ⓐ

2 Retrace the main outlines for a looser, relaxed look.

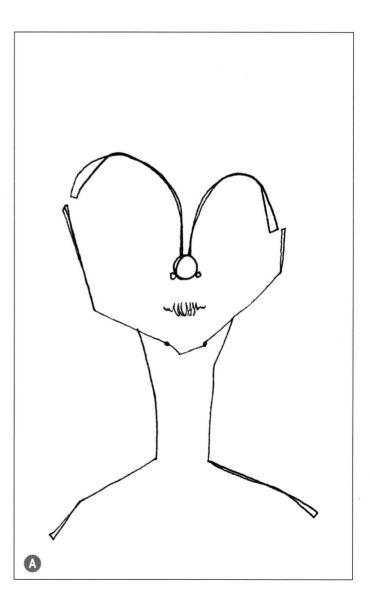

Ⓐ

3 Doodle the basic shapes of the eyes, ears, and antlers. Remember that antlers and ears are mirror images of of each other. **B**

4 Darken the outlines and add some shading with crosshatching, stripes, and diagonal lines. With a tight crosshatch, doodle fur on the ears and neck, and draw a V shape for the heart. **C**

5 Use colored pencils to draw freckles, cheeks, and other details as you like.

tip

Play around with different color combinations. You'll be surprised how much this woodland girl's mood and personality can change depending on her color!

132

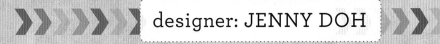
INKY Doodled Folders

DOODLE PROMPT: Learn to doodle with paint droppers, and customize your office accessories!

what you'll need

- Kraft file folders
- Black and white acrylic inks in dropper bottles
- Small paintbrush
- Small jar of water
- Vintage paper
- Scissors
- Glue stick

instructions

1 Use white acrylic ink in a dropper bottle to doodle wonky circles on the front cover of a kraft file folder. Ⓐ

2 Use a wet paintbrush to pull the ink into one of the circles to fill it in. Repeat with a few other circles, and let dry. Ⓑ

3 Use black acrylic ink with a dropper to doodle illegible text over the circles. Let dry. Ⓒ

4 Cut a piece of vintage paper to fit the tab portion of the folder, and attach it with a glue stick. Ⓓ

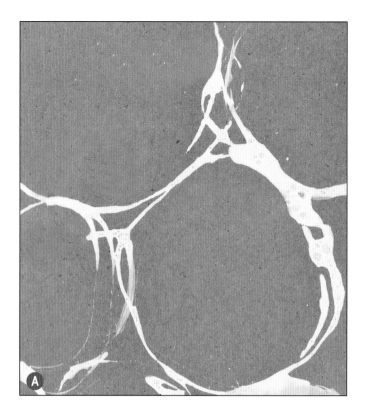

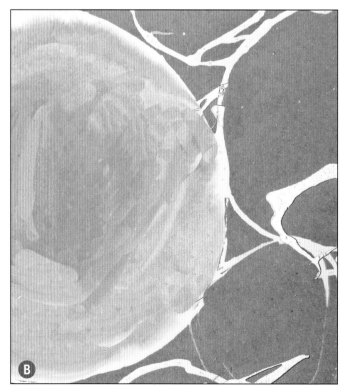

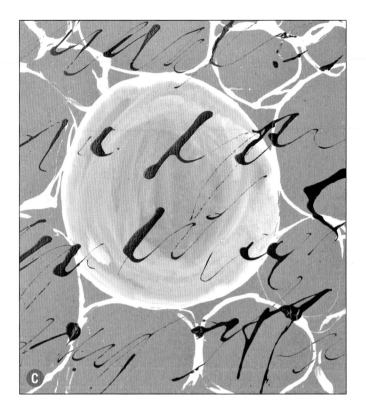

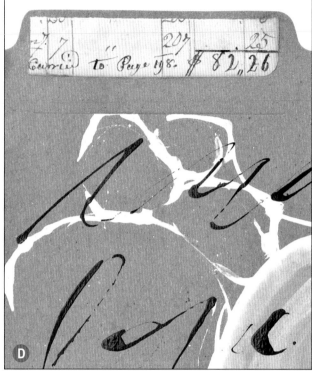

tip

If your acrylic ink does not come with a dropper bottle, you can buy droppers or pipettes separately online or use straws.

Rub and DOODLE

DOODLE PROMPT: In the first step of this creative exercise, use a crayon to rub imprints of coins onto a piece of paper. Then comes the really fun part—using your imagination to see patterns and images within the rubbings!

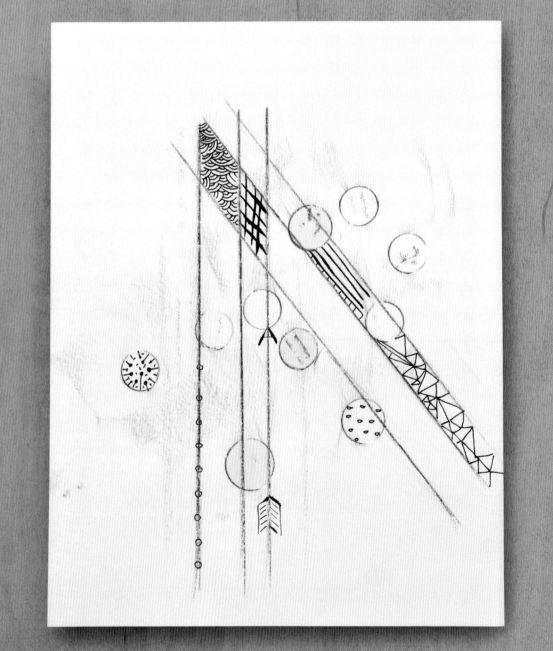

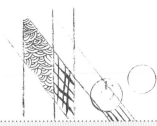

what you'll need

- Coins of various sizes
- Plain white paper
- Black crayon
- Black fine-point marker
- Markers in assorted colors

instructions

1 Gather coins and set them on your work surface.

2 Place a plain white piece of paper on top of the coins.

3 Rub the entire piece of paper with a black crayon. Ⓐ

4 Place the paper on top of a file folder and rub the paper with the crayon to make an imprint of a line. Repeat several times, moving the folder slightly each time to make additional imprints of lines at different angles.

5 Doodle within the rubbed marks by drawing small lines, circles, and scallops with a black fine-point marker.

6 Add splashes of color to some of the rubbed circles with markers.

Ⓐ

tip

There is no end to items that would be fun to rub with a crayon! Try a piece of crocheted lace with a red crayon, doodle circles around some of the rubbings, and connect the circles with lines for a finished piece that looks like a constellation of stars.

Jenny Doh

DOODLED
Vintage Photos

DOODLE PROMPT: Add color and personality to vintage photos with doodles!

what you'll need

- Vintage portrait photographs
- Paint markers in assorted colors

instructions

photo 1 Ⓐ

1 Use a red paint marker to doodle a circle onto the nose of a person in a vintage photograph.

2 Use a black paint marker to doodle circles and lines to make glasses. Add small dots on the glasses with a white paint marker.

3 Color in the background of the photo with a white paint marker.

4 Doodle other embellishments with paint markers in assorted colors.

Ⓐ

photo 2 Ⓑ

1 In a group portrait photograph, doodle an outline around the seated people with a white paint marker. Add small dots in the space outside of the silhouette.

2 Connect the white dots with a black paint marker. Make some lines solid and some lines dotted.

photo 3 Ⓒ

1 Outline the subject's clothing, such as a jacket and lapels, with a white paint marker.

2 Doodle glasses and a long nose onto the man's face with a black paint marker, and add white accents.

3 Doodle an umbrella and rain drops.

tips

- If you don't have vintage photographs, you can buy them on eBay or at antique stores.
- Use this same approach to doodle on any extra family photos that you have lying around.

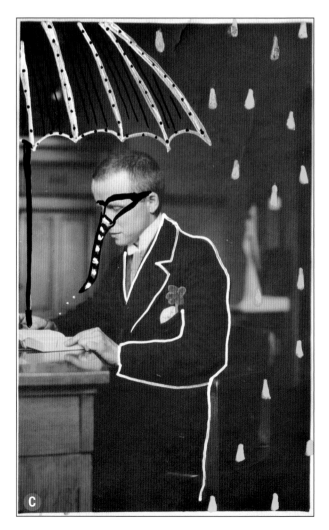

COTTON BALL Doodles

DOODLE PROMPT: Smudges made with an inkpad and a cotton ball turn into charming little doodles with just imagination and a pen.

try it

Dab a cotton ball onto a brown inkpad, and make smudges on a white piece of paper. Let dry, and then use a black fine-point pen to doodle whatever creatures and objects the smudges inspire. Doodle details such as polka dots and stripes to complete each doodle.

About the CONTRIBUTORS

Danita is a self-taught mixed-media artist living in El Paso, Texas. Danita is a self-proclaimed artist in motion because she's always looking for a new project to work on and a new medium to tackle. From art dolls and paper collages to acrylics and oils, she's done it all. To learn more, visit *www.danitaart.com*.

David Danell is a Stockholm-based artist who focuses his work on pen and ink drawings that combine elements of realism with figments of his imagination, for completely creative results. To learn more, visit *websta.me/n/daviddanell*.

Dino Perez is an urban creative living and working in Santa Ana, California, as a graphic designer. He fell in love with creating at an early age, often asking his parents for doodles of people, animals, and flowers before he could really draw himself. In his free time, Dino paints, illustrates, goes to movies, and loves taking pictures with an instant camera. To learn more, visit *www.dinoperez.com*.

Heidi Vandal lives and works in a tiny apartment in Odense, Denmark. When her family is out of the house, she paints, draws, and combines all different kinds of materials in paintings, illustrations, and art journals. She loves to teach art, create commissioned works of children, decorate walls, or do anything that pushes her out of her comfort zone to generate new ideas. To learn more, visit *www.heidivandal.dk*.

Jan Avellana is an artist, writer, mother of two boys, and wife to her sweetheart of 22 years. By day, she is an elementary school teacher in Hawaii, and by night, she draws and creates into the wee hours, all the while working toward her dream of being a full-time artist. To learn more, visit *www.janavellana.com*.

Javier Pérez Estrella, also known as cintascotch, is a graphic designer and audio-visual producer living in Guayaquil, Ecuador. His work, which he shares on various social media platforms under the name cintascotch, reflects the simple and minimal side of art as he combines everyday objects with simple, yet supremely clever doodles. To learn more, visit *www.javierperez.ws*.

Jen Osborn is a third-generation artist from rural Michigan who spends most of her time drawing, knitting, and sewing. Her work has been published in major craft magazines and books, including her own, *Mixed and Stitched: Fabric Inspiration for the Mixed-Media Artist*. To learn more, visit *themessynest.com*.

Jennifer Betlazar is a San Diego–based artist, jewelry boutique owner and curator, and creative consultant for a nationwide wholesale gift company. When she's not painting, embroidering, or doodling, she can be found traveling the world in search of inspiration and coffee. To learn more, find her on Instagram under the name LaDiDaDaDa.

Jennifer Mercede is a Portland, Oregon–based artist who thrives on creating pieces that are spontaneous, free, and fun. She enjoys using bright colors mixed with softer neutrals, and she loves drawing animals and then adding personality to them with off-beat colors. To learn more, visit *www.jennifermercede.com*.

Kate Gabrielle is a New Jersey–based self-taught illustrator and painter. When she's not drawing or painting, she enjoys dabbling in jewelry, reading books about the Middle Ages, and hanging out with her cats, Chloe and Arrietty. To learn more, visit *www.kategabrielle.com*.

Monika Forsberg is an artist and mother of two living by a river in London. She grew up by the sea in Sweden, and it's safe to say that water is one of her biggest inspirations. She loves creating playful, magical, technicolor fantasies. To learn more, visit *www.walkyland.com.*

Pam Garrison is an artist, crafter, and teacher who is passionate about creating and inspiring others to do the same. She lives in Southern California with her family and strives to make something every day. To learn more, visit *www.pamgarrison.com.*

Julia Grimm is a Germany-based artist and teacher who fell in love with art again at the age of 32, after a 20-year break. When she found her way in art again, drawing became instantly vital to her, and she hasn't stopped drawing since. She doodles to find that peaceful place that reminds her of drawing in her childhood. To learn more, visit *lineosa.wordpress.com.*

Stephenie Purl Hamen is a mixed-media artist, doodler, paper crafter, avid home cook and recipe writer, mother of two boys, and wife to her husband, Matt. Living in Sun Prairie, Wisconsin, she works every day to create a prettier, happier, and more beautiful world, and to teach others to do the same. To learn more, visit *www.thevintageprairie.com.*

Theo Ellsworth is a self-taught artist and comics creator widely known for his graphic novel *Capacity* and *Sleeper Car*, which was featured in *The Best American Comics 2010*. Hailing from Montana, Theo loves drawing and writing stories about the people that live in the imaginary places that he creates. To learn more, visit *www.thoughtcloudfactory.com.*

Lindsay Mason is a freelance artist, designer, and demonstrator living in Poulton, England. She designs her own line of stamps for the British company Personal Impressions, she is a certified Ranger Educator, and she wrote her own book, *Stamping*, in 2009. When she's not creating with paper, she enjoys gardening, the theater, and journaling. To learn more, visit *www.lindsaymason.blogspot.com.*

About the AUTHOR

Jenny Doh is head of *www.crescendoh.com* and also head of Studio Crescendoh, located in Santa Ana, California, where she teaches painting and fiber arts. She has authored and packaged numerous books including *More Creative Lettering, Creative Lettering, Craft-a-Doodle, Stamp It!, Journal It!, We Make Dolls!,* and, *Washi Wonderful.* She loves to create, stay fit, and play music.

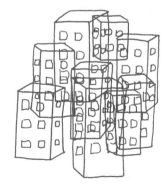